WHAT IS
JESUS?

DANIEL LEE

authorHOUSE®

AuthorHouse™ LLC
1663 Liberty Drive
Bloomington, IN 47403
www.authorhouse.com
Phone: 1-800-839-8640

Published by AuthorHouse   01/31/2014

ISBN: 978-1-4918-5754-0 (sc)
ISBN: 978-1-4918-5755-7 (e)

Library of Congress Control Number: 2014901961

Any people depicted in stock imagery provided by Thinkstock are models,
and such images are being used for illustrative purposes only.
Certain stock imagery © Thinkstock.

This book is printed on acid-free paper.

Because of the dynamic nature of the Internet, any web addresses or links contained in
this book may have changed since publication and may no longer be valid. The views
expressed in this work are solely those of the author and do not necessarily reflect the
views of the publisher, and the publisher hereby disclaims any responsibility for them.

Scripture quotations marked KJV are from the Holy Bible,
King James Version (Authorized Version).
First published in 1611. Quoted from the KJV Classic Reference Bible,
Copyright © 1983 by The Zondervan Corporation.

TABLE OF CONTENTS

FOREWORD

It is not my intent to give cause to dissention and / or offense to any one, any place in the world of any society or religious or spiritual belief. It is my hope and intent to provoke some deep thought and meditation concerning wide spread debates and hostilities involving some religions and the individual convictions about the person of Jesus the Christ. I hope that upon reading this book, many people will gain a refreshing awareness of cultural and philosophical differences and be more able to respect those differences in a warm spirit compared to a prejudiced attitude and mind set. Our most powerful and dangerous enemy hides within our own minds.

John Osteen wrote in his book: The Confessions of a Baptist Preacher (1983): "It will be recorded in history that ours has been one of the most turbulent, violent, and shocking generations that has ever lived upon the face of the earth."

Thirty years have since passed and I can see that history is being recorded as he so stated. We are in that time now.

DEDICATION

I dedicate the efforts and research making this composition available, to all peoples of every nation, my family, religious teachers and elders, and all journalists. My deepest respect and warmest wishes for the many teachers, mentors, friends, and associates who have been an inspiration to me throughout my life.

INTRODUCTION

Who am I ?

I feel great prudence in introducing myself to you. Many people around the world need to identify a certified degree title to an author of any literary publication. At this time, I have no college degree or academic portfolio. What I do have is memories, recollections, and years of thought as day after day I look and see the world we live in.

Though there are many, one of my greatest experiences throughout a twenty year career in the U.S. Navy was the privilege of knowing and spending time with numerous and very enlightened people of different religious committed beliefs.

Upon graduating High School in 1970, I left home and quickly steered myself away from the Catholic life I had inherited from birth. At that time it was adamantly taught to me that Catholics were blessed to be the one true Church, tracing their roots back to one of the original Apostles, named Peter. At that time, I was made to believe that looking at another church was a sin. To enter another church and/or participate with another church was immediate damnation. It wasn't until years later, that those of the Catholic faith took upon themselves a Christian affiliation.

I feel that a brief back ground of myself will help you the reader better understand what I will share with you in these following pages. After Graduating High School, I went to Business School and later joined the U.S. Navy in March 1973.

Throughout these pages, it will not be my purpose or intent to point or in any way attack or put down any philosophical or religious belief of the reader. My only intent and purpose is to ask one question. <u>What is JESUS?</u>

WHAT IS JESUS ?

From the beginning of the Bible Book of Genesis, those who say they are Christian will profess that the "Man" of the New Testament of the Bible is known by many names and titles.

Throughout the History of mankind, so much torture, persecution, mayhem, and slaughter has ensued on so many societies in His name and in the Name of the Father Creator over and of all things. The same has and continues to take place because of a common belief in an ALMIGHTY GOD.

This causes me great anxiety concerning perhaps the greatest question one may ask themselves. WHY? . . . Is "WHO" the root cause of all this chaos or is "WHAT" the well hidden & secret underlying justification?

As one studies the many religions of the world, one discovers that most religions have one common belief. That common belief is of one GOD over all things. "HE" who created all things and set an order concerning all things. With this common belief, why is there so much persecution and why have so many wars throughout time, been fought for the purpose of GOD and in the Name of JESUS? Have we all missed the most important message that has been given to us over and over and over again? I strongly believe we have.

For the sake of time, eternity, salvation, eternal rewards, universal and cosmic heaven and hell, and truth(?); How is it possible for so many different religions to exist and compete with one another?

TRUTH

What is "Truth"? Truth is that which reinforces itself. Truth will still be Truth across a spectrum of events or situations. Facts may or may not support a Truth. "There's a world of difference between truth and facts. Facts can obscure truth." (—Maya Angelou) Truth will always put a light on supporting facts.

A very strong similarity in the Christian Bible and the Quran is that History and Science validates many things in both. An example: History validates the Crucifixion of Jesus (Tacitus). History validates the demise of the Egyptian army at the Red Sea. Oceanic research confirms intact debris on the shallow underwater self of the Red Sea floor. Medical Science confirms that the mummified body of the Pharaoh of Egypt at that time did indeed die from drowning and physical body trauma (Bucaille 1994, 127).

It is Truth that the recorded testimonies of the many individuals that make up the Bible and the message of the Holy Prophet Muhammad, of the Quran, are confirmed time and time again, by History, Science, Anthropology, and Medicine as being accurate. Skeptics can diminish the accuracy of one detail or another in the Bible however, it is essential to be mindful that the Bible is a collection of individual testimonies given after the fact. Keep in mind the undeniable fact that a doctor will express a different view point of an event than would a blacksmith or a farmer.

Take a moment to consider this scenario: A doctor, blacksmith, and farmer are all three at the scene of an accident. Let's imagine there is fifty plus feet between each of them. Soon after the time of the accident, a police investigator takes statements from all three. As the investigator reviews the statements from each of the three, distinct differences are noticed in each of the statements. Does the investigator discard the statements or does he/she eagerly seek the truth resulting facts, within the three statements? This is the burden given to the truth seeking Christian and all others seeking the Truth about all teachings in the matters of God. Much of the Bible and the Torah was written after the fact, based on recollections.

The Quran stands undiminished in its entirety, as the only known and available original document about God. The greatest similarity of Jews, Judeo-Christians, Christians, and the people of Islam is this; All believe in one Supreme GOD.

RELIGION

It is very apparent that many religions do exist and strive in an endless battle of competition to recruit new members and exert their beliefs into the lives of others. These religions are categorized as outwardly focused religions.

The majority of these religions identify themselves as Christians. This makes Christianity the world's largest populated faith group to date. The Christian population can be sub-categorized into any one or more of the following groups: Anglicans, Catholics, Independents, Marginals, Orthodox, Protestants, Charismatics, Neo-charismatics, Pentecostals, and so many more.

According to Gordon-Conwell Theological Seminary, roughly 43,000 different Christian denominations existed worldwide in 2012. That is up from 500 in 1800 and 39,000 in 2008 and this number is expected to grow to 55,000 by 2025.

I can't begin to estimate the number of times I have heard "Christians" state that Muslims should self-govern themselves to prevent misunderstanding of the Quran, among themselves. Now evidence supports over 43,000 different Christian Doctrines? By the time you are reading this, I dread to think how many versions of the Bible will be published.

Studying the global picture of the differences between those who profess convictions to the Torah, those of the Bible, and those of the Quran, we discover that the list for the core differences is much shorter than the list of similarities.

What is Religion? A very simple explanation for defining Religion is: a specific fundamental set of beliefs and practices generally agreed upon by a number of persons or sects: ie:, Christian religion; the Buddhist religion, etc. The body of persons adhering to a particular set of beliefs and practices. Some examples are (BBC Religions):

- **Atheism** Atheists are people who believe that god or gods are man-made constructs.
- **Baha'i** One of the youngest of the world's major religions.
- **Buddhism** A way of living based on the teachings of Siddhartha Gautama.
- **Candomblé** A religion based on African beliefs, originating in Brazil.
- **Christianity** The world's biggest faith, based on the teaching of Jesus Christ.
- **Hinduism** A group of faiths rooted in the religious ideas of India.
- **Islam** Revealed in its final form by the Holy Prophet Muhammad.
- **Jainism** An ancient philosophy and ethical teaching that originated in India.
- **Jehovah's Witnesses** A Christian-based evangelistic religious movement.
- **Judaism** Based around the Jewish people's covenant relationship with God.
- **Mormonism** The Church of Jesus Christ of Latter-day Saints.
- **Paganism** Contemporary religions usually based on reverence for nature.
- **Rastafari** A young religion founded in Jamaica in the 1930s.
- **Santeria** Afro-Caribbean syncretic religion originating in Cuba.
- **Shinto** Japanese folk tradition and ritual with no founder or single sacred scripture.
- **Sikhism** The religion founded by Guru Nanak in India in the 15th Century CE.
- **Spiritualism** Spiritualists believe in communication with the spirits of people who have died.

- **Taoism** An ancient tradition of philosophy and belief rooted in Chinese worldview.
- **Unitarianism** An open-minded and individualistic approach to religion.
- **Zoroastrianism** One of the oldest monotheistic faiths, founded by the Prophet Zoroaster.

BBC.CO.UK

As we review the list above, we see several religion names ending with an "ism". Let's take a look at a few more words ending with an "ism":

Absenteeism	Activism	Agnosticism	Autoeroticism
Behaviorism	Capitalism	Catechism	Communism
Egalitarianism	Electromagnetism	Embolism	Exorcism
Fascism	Globalism	Hedonism	Hypnotism
Idealism	Imperialism	Journalism	Patriotism
Racism	Socialism	Tourism	Vandalism

All of these words are acts, actions, doctrines, or policies of Man's standards and/or positions. These are all terms, relating to the actions of man/humans. When we see any subject, action, and religion which is of an "ism", we know beforehand, that a requirement to pacify, edify, or otherwise meet man's approval will be present, or that the term specifies a physical action by man. In this description, meeting man's approval is synonymous with meeting the Church's approval/standard. Organized religions typify the "ism" complex, ie:, Catholicism, Lutheranism, Methodism, and Judaism. In my own experience, Catholicism is very apparent in that typically a reference will be made at least once during the Mass, concerning the blessings or approval of the Catholic Church and God. Inference to meeting the approval of the Catholic Church always precedes the need or requirement of meeting God's approval. Remember, Catholics were identified as one of the religion groups that identify themselves with being Christian. I ask myself this question: If the Catholic Church is a Christian Church, why don't Catholics carry their Bibles to Church? In my experience, Bible believing Christians enter a church service with their own personal Bible in hand. I am comfortably certain, GOD dealt with and established a direct open door relationship with mankind at Calvary. The Bible and Quran concur with a direct one-on-one connection with GOD. So, since the Bible and the Quran both concur and so many have experienced a direct connection or relationship with GOD, why would some organized Church try to convince so many, that one must meet the Church's approval before they may receive GOD's approval? If this is not the case, then do these religions imply that both the CHURCH and GOD are equal and must be in agreement for blessings and salvation to be awarded to an individual?

I have witnessed another surprising element about a number of Christian organized Churches. During the course of the service, the Priest and congregation recite (in monotone) a prayer known as the "Apostle's Creed". One of the lines in this prayer states: "I believe in the Holy Catholic Church". The immediate thoughts that slammed into my mind are: If you believe in the Holy Catholic Church, why are you set apart from the Catholic Church? How do you support the Catholic Church? Why do you so closely mimic the Catholic service? What is it about the Catholic Church you believe in? All of this separation, drama, and confusion makes me truly ponder what exactly do so many diverse and inconsistent Christians and religions actually believe? One of the things that is so insanely amazing is the anger that erupts when one starts talking about the wonders of GOD and Jesus. Many individuals do not want to hear it! Christians (obviously self-proclaimed) who become enraged about studying and hearing the Word of GOD? What percentage of the so called Christian community, do these people make up? Could it be a greater percentage then the five percent that make up the the groups that governments have identified as Muslim terrorist? When cultures, governments, and societies talk bad about Christians, which group of the more than 43,000 Christian groups are they referring to? When people talk bad about Muslims, which group of Muslims are they talking about? Who other than legions of demons would benefit from pitting GOD focused people against each other?

BIBLE GAP

Has no one noticed a 15 year gap in the life of Jesus, as reported in the New Testament of the Bible? Has no one noticed the evidence of selfish pride among the 12 Apostles as recorded in the New Testament of the Bible? First, let's look at one case of selfish pride being reported. I will refer to Mark 9:38(KJ), "And John answered him, saying, Master, we saw one casting out devils in thy Name, and he followeth not us, and we forbade him, because he followeth not us." Mark was witness to a conversation between John and Jesus. "But Jesus said, Forbid him not, for there is no man, which shall do a miracle in my Name, that can lightly speak evil of me. For he that is not against us, is on our part."

It is undeniable that the twelve original Apostles believed that they alone were given authority to use the power of GOD's authority through Jesus. We can paraphrase verse 38: We saw a stranger casting out demons in Your Name. He is not one of us! Jesus responded to John and those present with Him: Don't worry about others who are doing works in My Name! What a POWERFUL statement! Was Jesus saying: Learn, Practice, and Live what I tell you?

I made mention of a 15 year gap in the Bible chronology of the life of Jesus. As you read the New Testament, you may notice that at the approximate age of twelve, Jesus was teaching in the Synagogues. When He approached the river where John the Baptist was on that one day, we discover that Jesus is the approximate age of 30. I mention the approximate age of 30 because it is debated as to whether Jesus was age 27 or age 30 on that day. From the approximate age of 12 until the age of 27, fifteen years has elapsed. What did He do during that time?

Why may this have happened? Let us reflect on the Hebrew customs and traditions of that time. When a boy entered his teen years, his family would choose a wife for him to marry. According to prophesy as given in the Old Testament, marriage did not fit into the time and ministry of Jesus. If He had taken a wife, would she have been a widow fifteen to eighteen years later, and numerous children who's father suddenly abandoned them? Would that have been an example of GOD's love to have His earth family having all the goodness ripped from them as their dad was being tortured and hung on the cross, naked for the world to see?

Therefore, Jesus left His clan (if you will) and went off on His own. Why would we even consider, He would go into hiding and never have contact with any one? He was commissioned to dwell among men. Let us remember His ministry time frame. It will have significance later. From the age of twelve when He was teaching in the Temples and Synagogues, until the age of thirty or maybe thirty three when he was Crucified, is as much as twenty one years.

Perhaps the many letters and documents selectively omitted from the Bible, by various councils in the early beginnings of the Catholic Church and earlier gave evidence of those fifteen years. The world may never know for certain. Historians do agree that the Bible was written over a period of 1,600 years (Bible Facts). How many letters have never been read and given consideration for inclusion in the Bible we know? How many scrolls of testimony and reports have been hidden from scholars and publishers for inclusion in the Bible? How many pages of writings have been condensed down to a greatly reduced number of Bible pages? Weighing these considerations, what measure of wisdom and enlightenment allows for the critical critiquing of a minute number of perceived errors, in the Bible?

THE MANY NAMES OF GOD

Looking at the many names of GOD in the Hebrew list and the English Bible list, we find there are many names for GOD/Jesus. Many of the names listed are phrase names, such as "The One Who Gives Peace". Many of the Names pertaining to GOD, come from the numerous versions of the Bible, ie; King James, New King James, International Version, New International Version, New American Standard, New Life Version, New Living Translation, New Revised Standard Version, Anglicized, New Century Version, and more — plus translations and interpretations for an endless number of other languages.

When we investigate the Islamic List of Names for GOD, we find exactly 99 and one unknown unspeakable Name. This is attributed to the apparent fact that the Islamic Names come from one original Quran. This is most unique in that the original Quran is written in High Arabic. The words of High Arabic have one meaning and one meaning only. This differs greatly from the many applications and contextual uses of words in other languages. It is conclusively undeniable that the GOD of the Torah, the Bible, and the Quran are one and the same GOD. (Refer to Appendix A and B)

PROPHET MUHAMMAD

We have learned from the Bible that Jesus came to dwell among us in fulfillment of an age old prophesy. Scrutinized investigation of prophetic and historical timelines confirms that no other person could have possibly appeared in the place of Jesus. He was the one and only that fit in the prophetic timeline. Everything was synchronized for his coming. I do mean everything. Everything right down to the location of the thorn bush that was pruned to be woven and shaped for his tormenting crown, the tree that was cut and cleaned to make up the cross that held him suspended for his physical death. And so many more.

In those hours leading up to His arrest in the Garden of Gethsemane and until His last breath on the cross, it is made clear that even though He was One with GOD, He was separate from GOD. This is most evident in **Luke 22:42**

> "Saying, Father, if thou be willing, remove this cup from me: nevertheless not my will, but thine, be done"; and **Mark 15:34**" And at the ninth hour Jesus cried with a loud voice, saying, Eloi, Eloi, lama sabachthani? which is, being interpreted, My God, my God, why hast thou forsaken me?" (KJ)

Clearly, this is the fearful and anguished human element of the person of Jesus. This is very crucial in understanding the intense, complex and divine dynamics of the person of Jesus. More on this will be discussed later. We previously mentioned that Jesus went about fulfilling His mission here on earth between the age of twelve and approximately age thirty. Pushing beyond critical semantics, He went in to overdrive, so to speak, between age twenty seven and age thirty. Most importantly, He traveled and taught the way, the wisdom, and the WORD of GOD for three years. The relevant point is this: From age twelve until His arrest, whether at age thirty or age thirty three, His ministry period was fifteen to eighteen years. This contemplation will soon became apparent.

Let's leap forward in time to 570 A.D., in the city of Mecca, located on the Arabian Peninsula, approximately 50 miles inland from the Red Sea port city of Jidda (Jedda), a new born infant is given the name Muhammad. Muhammad's genealogy leads back to Ishmael, the first born of Abraham and His Wife's maiden named Hagar. Abraham was told by GOD that Ishmael would be at odds with many and that many would be at odds with him. Plainly stated, Ishmael would live by the sword. Evidence strongly indicates that when Abraham's wife, Sara, sent Hagar and Ishmael out of Abraham's clan, they eventually ended up traveling the deserts of what is now known as western Saudi Arabia. History also states that Hagar remarried, and had children by her husband. History also shows that following this time frame, numerous battles ensued between a Tribe group known as the Hagarites and Roman Armies. In Psalm 83, several tribe names are mentioned including the Ishmaelites. Bible history strongly indicates the tribes of the desert were nomadic and very strong, swift, and sure fighters. We know that Hagar had more sons and we know Ishmael had sons. The names of Ishmael's sons correlate with the names of Tribes, cities, and regions of the history of that time. Perhaps Hagar's husband moved Hagar and Ishmael from western Arabia to Eastern Arabia however, my point in this is to state that it is very possible that Ishmael could have erected an alter in the then camp site that became known as Mecca. This gives validity to Prophet Muhammad's claim that Ishmael constructed the Alter (Kabala) that helps establish Mecca as a Holy City for the people of Islam (Muslims). Prophet Muhammad's whole ancestry was nomadic traders of camels, horses, spices, incense, and fine cloths. This was the greater culture up and beyond the Crusades which took place years later. At some point back in time, we know that a great number of the cities, local governments, and Nomadic tribes were Pagans and Hedonist, as stated in the Bible testament of Sodom and Gomorra. This greatly increases the significance of Prophet Muhammad's future.

At the approximate age of twenty six, the Prophet Muhammad married. He was perhaps the only man in the greater Arabic territory that had or desired one wife only, as the society at large was very polygamous. Records indicate that the Prophet Muhammad sought something more than the mundane repetitive life that encompassed him. One day while out and about and whether by exploratory luck or divine guidance, he discovered an entrance to a cave, which once inside was a totally relaxing space of peaceful isolated solitude. In 610 A.D., at the age of 40, the future Prophet Muhammad experienced the first of many visits from GOD's Messenger Angel, Gabriel. Thus the birth of the Quran. This continued for the next twenty two years. Compare this to Jesus' ministry life. Perhaps as much as three years into these revelations, he started telling close friends about what was being given to him. Soon, others were gathering with him. As happened to Jesus, He and those close to him became targets of persecution, from the Pagan polytheistic population. Everybody was living happy and lecherous lives, and the rising Prophet Muhammad was starting to cause them offense. So much so that divine intervention woke him one night to flee Mecca in order to escape assassination. (Remember Mary and Joseph's exodus from Bethlehem?)

The Prophet Muhammad travelled to a city that was later named Al-Medina (the illuminated city). Ten years later, he had spoken in High Arabic, which was not in his knowledge to do, to a Christian Priest Scribe who wrote his words in High Arabic to produce the Quran. By this time, Islam had spread across Arabia becoming a major standard and force to be reckoned with. For 1400 years, Islam has continued to inspire citizens of the World. Statisticians project that Islam will soon over take the combined Christian network of affiliations, to become the largest population society in the world.

THE SON OF GOD

After much research and thought, I discovered an essay concerning and explaining many concepts of word association, social meanings, and relationship characterizations of the term "Son" with respect to the Bible and the many statements about the "SON of GOD". I do believe it covers many valid view points about the prophecy of and the birth of the "SON of GOD."

This essay was captured in its entirety from http://www.answering-islam.org/Hahn/son.html August 4, 2013

"Jesus as the Son of God

by

Luther Engelbrecht
Ernest Hahn

Introduction

Muslims believe that God is one, that there are no gods except the God. They may contend that even though Christians claim to be monotheists, they actually believe in more than one God. Since

Christians believe that Jesus is the Son of God, they therefore err like other people of ancient or modern times who have believed in a plurality of gods or the sons and daughters of God.

So often Muslim-Christian religious discussion breaks on the topic of Jesus' Sonship. The Christian affirms that Jesus is the Son of God; the Muslim denies that Jesus is the Son of God. Both simply agree to disagree, each convinced that he is right and the other is wrong, as they go their separate ways.

But is there another alternative? In suggesting that there is, the following questions are proposed: Has the Christian truly understood what Jesus' Sonship means to the Muslim and why the Muslim rejects it? Has the Muslim truly understood what Jesus Sonship means to the Christian and why the Christian affirms it? On this topic, which for centuries has been notorious for generating more heat than light, could both agree to explain their relative positions more fully and to listen to one another more intently and courteously?

The intention of this essay is to help both Muslims and Christians to penetrate a little deeper into the Biblical concept of Jesus as the Son of God and the significance of this idea for Christians. At the same time, it is hoped that this essay, as it unfolds, demonstrates at least some sensitivity towards a truly Muslim position on this vital topic. Where it needs correction or amplification, gladly let Muslim friends provide it.

Biblical Meaning of "Son"

To understand the Biblical meaning of Jesus as "the Son of God", first we must examine the Biblical use of the word "son". In the Bible, "son" is a term expressing an intimate relationship with someone or something; basically, it indicates origin, but it is also used to express close association or identification with persons or things. Even when indicating origin, this term does not limit oneself to one's father and mother. One may be called the "son" of the following: his father and mother, his family, his tribe, his people, his place of birth (city or country), and the time or circumstance of his birth. The if "father-son" terminology is also used in connection with kings and their vassals or subjects, masters and servants, teachers and disciples, and almost any situation in which someone is subordinate to or dependent on someone else. The basic requirement of the "son" is to honour and obey his "father", but he should also love him and emulate him.

The term "son" is used in many other ways in the Bible, some of which are connected with origin but others of which mainly express some sort of association with or resemblance to persons or things. A large, somehow homogeneous group may be called "sons" (occupational and ethnic groups especially). Sometimes characteristics or qualities themselves are personified and regarded as having "sons"— those who possess that same characteristic or quality. Still also other uses of the term "son" in the Bible reflect the versatile and imaginative use of this term especially in the Hebrew language.

A complete list of the various uses of the term "son" in the Bible would be too long for this essay. A few of its more idiomatic uses are listed below, with their literal meanings and the translations of the Holy Bible, New International Version (or The New English Bible or Holy Bible, Revised Standard Version).

Old Testament

Reference:	Expression (as literally in the original text) —Meaning (as found in the translation)
Genesis 5:32:	"son of five hundred years" —"five hundred years old"
Genesis 15:3:	"a son of my house" —"a servant in my household"
Deuteronomy 25:2:	"a son of stripes" —"deserves to be beaten"
Judges 19:22:	"sons of Belial" —"wicked men"
I Samuel 20:31:	"a son of death" —"he must die"

I Kings 20:35:	"sons of the prophets"
	—"a company of prophets" (NEB)
II Kings 14:14:	"sons of pledging"
	—"hostages"
Job 41:28:	"son of a bow"
	—"arrow" (NEB)
Isaiah 60: 10:	"sons of a foreign land"
	—"foreigners"
Lamentations 3:13:	"sons of a quiver"
	—"arrows from his quivers"
Joel 3:6:	"sons of the Grecians"
	—"the Greeks"
Zechariah 4:14:	"sons of oil"
	—"anointed"

New Testament

Matthew 9:15:	"sons of the bridegroom"
	—"the guests of the bridegroom"
Matthew 12:27:	"your sons"
	—"your people"
Luke 10:6:	"a son of peace"
	—"a man of peace"
Luke 16:8:	"the sons of this age"
	—"the people of this world";
	"the sons of lights"
	—"the people of the light"
John 17:12:	"the son of destruction"
	—"the one doomed to destruction"
Acts 13:26:	"sons of the family of Abraham"
	—"you who come of the stock of Abraham" (NEB)

Galatians 3:7:   "those who believe are children of Abraham"

Ephesians 2:2:   "the sons of disobedience"

                     —"those who are disobedient"

The above are only a few of the many uses of the term "son(s)" in the Holy Bible. The most common uses, which are usually translated literally, have been omitted. However, one such group might be illustrated here: personal, yet non-physical, Father-son" relationships:

	Father	Son(s)
I Samuel 3:6	Eli	Samuel
I Samuel 24:16	Saul	David
I Samuel 25:8	Nabal	David
Proverbs 1:8, etc.	Solomon	the reader
II Kings 2: 12	Elijah	Elisha
II Kings 8:9	Elisha	King Ben-Hadad
II Kings 5:13	Naaman	his servants
Judges 18:19	the priest	the people
Genesis 4:20f.	first musician	all musicians, etc
Matthew 9:2	Jesus	the paralytic
I Timothy 1:2, etc.	Paul	Timothy
Titus 1:4	Paul	Titus
Philemon 10	Paul	Philemon
I Peter 5: 13	Peterc	Mark

Other languages also use the term "son" in a variety of ways. Thus, in the Arabic language of the Qur'an "son" need not mean only a direct male issue or descendant. A familiar example is *ibnu's sabil* ("son of the road"), which means "a traveller". Another example with which many are familiar is "the son of Satan" a vivid descriptive for any mischief-maker (cf. also Acts 13:10). Obviously Satan does not have a wife in order to have a son! The name implies that the mischief maker is like Satan, an embodiment of Satan, a "Satan with us". Worthy of remembrance is also the Arabic term *ummu'l kitab* (literally "the mother of the book") the heavenly Scripture from which all Scripture with us on earth is derived, as if each Scripture were her child.

In the light of the above, let us turn to well known verses of the Qur'an: "He is Allah, the One . . . . He begetteth not nor was begotten . . . ." (Pickthall, The Meaning of the Glorious Koran, surah 112:1-4). This surah clearly states that God has no son and that no son can be God. Why? "How can He have a child, when there is for Him no consort? . . ." (surah 6:102). As these and other verses suggest, even to imagine that God would have a wife and sexual intercourse with her would be absolute folly. But do these Quranic verses actually address the Biblical meaning of Jesus' Sonship? Does the Bible affirm that God has a wife and through procreation a son, whose name is Jesus? Our response to these questions will become more intelligible after we consider in greater depth the Biblical meaning of "son of God".

Biblical Meaning of "Son of God"

The term "son of God" too is used in a variety of ways in the Holy Bible. As creator, God is the "Father" of Adam and of all mankind (Luke 3:38; Isaiah 64:8; Malachi 2:10; etc.). However, a more specific "Father-son" relationship is achieved by the gracious choice of the Father and the faithful obedience and service of the son, not by creation and certainly not by procreation. In this sense, the following are some of those referred to as "son(s) of God" in the Bible:

1. The people chosen by God (Exodus 4:22f.; Jeremiah 31:9,20; Hosea 11:1; Romans 8:14; II Corinthians 6:18; Galatians 3:26; Hebrews 2:10; Revelation 21:7)
2. Heavenly beings (Job 1:6)
3. Kings and rulers (II Samuel 7:14; Psalm 2:7; 82:6; 89:26f.)
4. Pious, godly individuals (Matthew 5:9; Luke 6:35)

If the meaning of the term "Son of God" in the case of Jesus would be limited to the same significance that it has in these cases above, even the Muslims might agree with its use. In fact, some Sufis speak of God as "Father" and humanity as "God's children". Other Muslims, of course, might question this terminology, preferring the use of "servant" instead of "son". Still, the fact remains that God being Father and humanity being His children, apart from any sexual connotation, is an idea compatible with the thinking of some Muslims.

To equate the Sonship of Jesus with the sonship of the above mentioned beings, however, would be denying the plain truth of the Holy Bible and the very essence of the Christian faith. Jesus is more than one of God's chosen people, more than one of His heavenly messengers, more than one who rules on God's behalf on earth, more than one who pleases God, although He is all of those also.

Jesus as the Unique Son of God

What, then, is the evidence for this tremendous claim? Is it because Jesus, though a man born of a woman, was yet born of a virgin? Some Christians, it is true, might conclude that because Jesus was born of the virgin Mary, therefore He is the Son of God. Likewise, some Muslims, while denying that Jesus is the Son of God, might consider the virgin birth of Jesus to be the basis for Christian belief that Jesus is the Son of God. Biblically speaking, however, Jesus' Sonship does not rest upon His being born of the virgin Mary. On the contrary, as we shall later see more clearly, His virgin birth rests upon His Sonship. Before Mary ever was, the Son of God is. Jesus does not become the Son of God, but the Son of God becomes Jesus. Thus Jesus, as the Son, speaks to the Father about "the glory I had with You before the world began" (John 17:5; cf. Colossians 1:13-20), long before Mary ever was. This eternal Son of God entered into the limitations of time and space by the power of God working through the virgin Mary and was born as a man, called Jesus, in Bethlehem some nineteen centuries ago.

Similarly, Jesus is not the Son of God because of His mighty works and wonderful words. On the contrary, He does His mighty works and speaks His wonderful words because He is the Son of God.

True, both the manner of Jesus' birth and the nature of His works lend evidence for His Sonship. But neither, alone or together, provides the origin or basis for His Sonship. The distinction is important.

Indeed, His works witness to His Sonship. A "son" must be obedient to his "father", doing his will and works, being like him (cf. John 8:37-47). Jesus Himself pointed to His works as evidence of the fact that He is the Son of God: "If I am not acting as my Father would, do not believe me. But if I am, accept the evidence of my deeds, even if you do not believe me, so that you may recognise and know that the Father is in me, and I in the Father" (John 10:37f.). Jesus did the works of God, His Father, acting as God would.

In addition to the evidence of His works, Jesus had other proof that He is **the** Son of God. At important times in His life, He was called the Son of God by the Father Himself and by others:

1. The Annunciation: The angel Gabriel told the virgin Mary that her son would be called "the Son of God". (Luke 1:32,35)
2. The Baptism: God's voice from heaven proclaimed: This is my Son, whom I love." (Matthew 3:17, etc.)
3. The Transfiguration: God's voice once again proclaimed: "This is my Son, whom I love. Listen to Him." (Mark 9:7, etc.)
4. The Crucifixion: The Roman centurion and his men confessed at the time of Jesus' crucifixion: "Surely he was the Son of God!" (Matthew 27:54)
5. The Resurrection: St. Paul writes that Jesus' resurrection from the dead declared Him to be "the Son of God". (Romans 1 :4)

Others in addition to God Himself, His angel, and the Roman soldier proclaimed that Jesus is the Son of God. Madmen and even unclean spirits confessed to Jesus: "You are the Son of God." (Mark 3:11; cf. 5:7; Matthew 8:29; Luke 4:41; 8:28). Jesus' disciples also confessed that He is "the Christ (Messiah), the Son of the living God" (Matthew 16:16; cf. 14:33). Jesus, as a true Son, preferred to give glory to His Father, but He too would not deny His Sonship (Matthew 26:63f.; Mark 14:62; John 10:36). Of interest in the first two of these passages (and others) is the close association between the terms "Messiah" and "Son of God".

It is also interesting to note how closely Jesus' Sonship is associated with His suffering (Romans 5:10; 8:32; Galatians 2:20; Hebrews 5:8; 6:6). When Jesus was famished after a long fast, the tempter said to Him: "If you are the Son of God, tell these stones to become bread" (Matthew 4:3, etc.). When Jesus was in agony on the cross, the passersby mocked Him and said: "Come down from the cross, if you are the Son of God!" (Matthew 27:40). These speakers forgot that Jesus is the Son of **God**. God, who seeks and serves and even suffers to save those whom He loves, the people of the world. He is not the son of some earthly king, who must show his might and save his pride by appearing to be victorious in the eyes of the world, according to the world's standards. It was just because He is the Son of the God of love that He would **not** use His power for selfish purposes but perfectly fulfilled the will of His Father, who chose to reveal Himself and His love to all men through His suffering Servant/Son.

Even a casual reading of the verses cited above would show that the use of the term "Son of God" with reference to Jesus is different in both quality and extent from the other uses mentioned previously. Others were graciously chosen by God as His adopted sons; the Son is in the Father eternally. Others obeyed the Father, though imperfectly; Jesus the Son obeyed Him perfectly, without sin (Hebrews 4:15). Sons should be like their father, but only Jesus was perfect like Him in His goodness, giving Himself completely for Him and His people. The Father has entrusted all judgement to the Son alone, "that all may honour the Son just as they honour the Father" (John 5:22,23). Only the Son gives life as the Father gives life (John 5:21). For was the Father has life in Himself, so He has granted the Son to have life in Himself" (John 5:26). The Son is obedient to the Father, with the will of the Father becoming concretized in the way of the Son; but the Father also listens and gives heed to the Son (John 11:41-44). Thus there is a sharing of power, authority, knowledge, glory, and kingship which indicates a relationship of equality and mutuality between the Two who are One. About what people, what angel, what king, what pious man could it be said: "In these last days God has spoken to us by the Son whom He has appointed heir of all things, and through whom He made the universe. The Son is the radiance of God's glory and the exact representation of His being, sustaining all things by His powerful word"? (Hebrews 1:2f.)

Many of the uses of the term "son" in the Holy Bible and in various languages can give clues to the significance of the term "Son of God" with reference to Jesus, but in the end its use, directly applied to Jesus, remains as unique as the relationship it expresses is unique. Jesus said: "I and the Father are one." (John 10:30)

Explaining the Meaning of Jesus as Son of God

How then, can Muslims (and Christians?) be helped to understand Jesus and the true significance of His name "Son of God"?

In the first place, it is significant that the Holy Injil does not portray Jesus indiscriminately proclaiming that He is the Son of God—and, for that matter, that He is the Messiah (Christ). Nor need we, especially when we know the term to be offensive to those with whom we converse. When we use it, we should explain it.

The Jews, in fact, were familiar with the title "Son of God", as they were familiar with the title "Messiah". There is evidence, though outside of the Bible, that they spoke about the Torah as the "daughter of God", meaning "the revelation of God", without sacrificing their monotheistic convictions. They did, however, object when Jesus called Himself "the Messiah" and "the Son of God", considering His confession of Himself to be blasphemy and worthy of crucifixion (John 5:18; cf. 10:33). It, therefore, is hardly surprising that Jesus Himself used this term discreetly.

Secondly, it should be made clear that Jesus was a man, a servant and a prophet, just as Muslims have always insisted and just as the Holy Injil claims the Son of God to have become. When the disciples of Jesus first met Jesus, they understood Him to be a man. How could they have understood otherwise? They had heard how Satan tempted Him. They saw Him hungry and weary. They knew Him in need of companionship and prayer. They saw Him weep. They heard Him in prayer and saw Him in action surrendering His will to the Father's will, claiming the Father's will to be His bread. His words: "The Father is greater than I" were intelligible to them. How else should they have understood? Or we, had we been with Him on earth?

Only after the disciples' association with Jesus had deepened, after they heard His words and witnessed His deeds, did they and others begin to wonder and ask questions about Him: "Who is this man?" "From where does He come?" They saw Him feed the multitudes, heal the sick, control nature, raise the dead. They heard Him forgive sins, they heard Him speak in an extraordinary manner about His purpose in coming, about His relation with the Temple, the Law and the prophets, about the love of God and His personal relationship with God. Even then, there were those who misinterpreted Him and His works, willfully or otherwise.

The disciples' understanding of both Jesus and His ministry was a gradual and at times a painful process. What He required of them to understand Him was not simply keen intellect but firm trust in God and obedience to His will, readiness for self-examination, repentance, and a change of mind and heart in the light of God's holiness and His holy Law, an openness to receive what He said about Himself, what He had done, what He was about to do, and the purpose of it all. True, Peter confessed Jesus to be the Messiah and Son of God, but immediately proceeded to contradict Jesus by denying that Jesus must suffer and die (Matthew 16:21,22), as if he had sharper insight into the will and ways of God than Jesus (John 12:1-7)! Women seemed to understand better (Mark 14:1-9). In brief, to understand Jesus is not simply to verbally confess Him, to admire and to applaud Him; it is to follow and obey Him.

In fact, the Holy Injil clearly and consistently indicates that Jesus' disciples did not fathom the deeper significance of His Sonship or His ministry until He had risen from the dead! Then their change in mind and heart was dramatic. Does this offer the Christian a clue for his witness? While to legislate techniques for presenting Jesus to the

Muslim or anyone may be dubious, is there here a 'procedural pattern on which Christians might meditate, even imitate?

Thirdly, it is often necessary to explain what the term "Son of God" in reference to Jesus does **not** mean. As already noted above, nowhere does the Holy Injil suggest that God takes Mary as a wife, that He procreates, and that Jesus therefore is the Son of God by virtue of His birth to Mary. God is no male deity! The Injil, like the Qur'an, speaks of Jesus as the son of the **virgin** Mary. In Arabic Jesus is called *ibnu'llah* not *waladu'llah*. Nor does the Injil sacrifice the fundamental Biblical affirmation that God is one. Nor does it suggest that somehow for Christians Jesus, as the Son of God, is another god associated with God, or that somehow Jesus, as the Son of God, is the second or third of three gods, or that somehow Jesus is elevated from His original position of man and servant to the status of the Son of God and then made to supplant the true God. In no way does the Holy Injil's affirmation of Jesus' Sonship transform Biblical monotheism into a subtle form of polytheism. God is one! And Jesus, the Son of God, confirms that God is one! Only **after** Muslims and Christians have established this common ground, can they proceed to discussion about who the one God is, what He does for mankind, what He expects from mankind, and how God is one while Jesus is the Son of God.

Fourthly, Christian belief in Jesus as the Son of God simply echoes the constant, insistent and consistent affirmation throughout the Injil that He is the Son of God. Contrary to what some Muslims suggest, normally with no evidence, Christians, including St. Saul, did not invent this title. For Christians to deny the Sonship of Jesus would mean that they should expunge all references in the Holy Injil to this title. If Christians were to do this, then they would be truly guilty of corrupting their Scriptures, just as many Muslims (but **not** the Qur'an) have felt Christians to have done. The Qur'an tells Christians that they are to judge according to the Injil (surah 5:46,47). It contains no reference to a corrupted or abrogated Injil.

Fifthly, and closely related to the previous points, Christians should encourage Muslims to read the Holy Injil with an open mind and heart and to compare both the Quranic and Biblical portrayals of Jesus' Sonship. Even if the Muslim rejects the Biblical portrayal of Jesus' Sonship after having seriously studied it, he should at least have understood the meaning of Jesus' Sonship as the Bible portrays it. Would the Muslim, after understanding the Biblical meaning of Jesus' Sonship, then entertain the possibility that the Quranic and Biblical portrayals of Jesus as the Son of God differ from each other, that the Qur'an rejects a concept of Jesus' Sonship which the Bible never affirms and could never affirm because it is really alien to the Biblical concept? Yet the Bible affirms Jesus to be the Son of God—in the **Biblical** sense of this term!

A frame of reference more congenial to the Islamic portrayal of Jesus may further help Muslims in understanding Jesus as the Son of God. Among the many names used of Jesus in the Qur'an, three especially can help elucidate the Christian understanding of His Sonship:

1. **'Abdu'llah** —"Servant of God" (surah 19:30)
2. **Rasulu'llah**—"Apostle (messenger) of God" (surah 4:157)
3. **Kalimatu'llah** —"word of God" (surah 4:171)

1. The prime duty of a son is to honour and obey his father, to serve him freely and fully. The ideas of being a servant and a son are very closely related in the Holy Bible. The Christian Church has always regarded the great Servant Songs in the book of the prophet Isaiah as referring to Jesus the Messiah (Isaiah 42:1-4; 52:13-53:12, etc.). This Servant is called "my chosen One" by God. "The Spirit of the Sovereign Lord" is upon Him (Isaiah 61:1). He heals the sick and helps the oppressed. He even suffers and bears the guilt of others and is vindicated by God. The early Christians used the same word found in the Servant Songs and referred to Jesus as God's "holy Servant" (Acts 4:27,30). This Son indeed served the Father, not out of compulsion but because of His unity with the Father and out of love. Which servant serves better than a son? In Jesus, the son and servant are fused!

2. An apostle or messenger is "one sent" by God to proclaim His message. Jesus also is called an "apostle" in the Holy Injil (Hebrews 3:1). In the Gospel account according to John, the Son is very often spoken of as "the sent One", and the two terms are almost synonymous. The other Gospel accounts use this terminology also, and the terms "Father" and "the sending One" are virtually synonymous too (Matthew 10:40; Mark 9:37: Luke 9:48). There have been many apostles who were sent by God. But the Apostle/Son was not only sent by God; He was also sent from God. He came forth from above, **from** God Himself (John 8:23,42) and so He is called "**Immanu-el**", "God with us". (Matthew 1:23)

Jesus' parable of the absent landlord is very instructive in the whole matter of His Sonship. The landlord's servants were unable to collect the rent for the vineyard he had planted and fully equipped and then let out to tenants. Finally, the landlord decided to send his son as his personal representative. The tenants killed him, thinking that thereby they had achieved victory and could take possession of the estate for themselves, but in the end they lost everything. (Matthew 21:33-43, etc.)

Plainly enough, the landlord and the son of the landlord in this parable represent the Father and the Son respectively. Whatever else the parable teaches, it clearly distinguishes between "the sent ones" and "the sent One," the prophets and the Son, and the ultimate destiny of "the sent One." Indeed, this parable is strange and unusual! Yet it is no stranger or more unusual than the Person and event to which the parable points.

Thus, it is clear for what purpose the Son has been sent by and from the Father: to reveal Him, to carry out His plan of salvation for mankind, to serve as His "personal" representative, and to expend Himself in the process (John 3:16f.; Romans 8:3,29; Galatians 4:4-7). In carrying out God's saving will, the unique Son was to acquire many "brothers", who, by following Him, also became God's "sons" by His gracious adoption. Those who follow the obedient Servant/Son sent from the Father are also God's obedient servants/sons, true "muslims" (as the followers of Jesus are called in the Qur'an—surah 3:52; 5:111).

Son/Servant/sent One/Saviour: all these are closely connected in the Holy Bible.

3. For Muslims, as for Christians, the Word of God is eternal, even as God is eternal. It is through His Word that God acts, creating and sustaining the universe and revealing His will. If one should refer to the Word of God among Muslims, they would naturally think of the Qur'an. However, many of them know that Jesus also is called "the word (Word?) of God" in the Qur'an. Even though they regard Jesus as only a prophet, could not their idea about His being "the word of God" be filled with the Biblical significance of the same expression? Some will say, "No!" Others have found this a very useful means for explaining Jesus' relationship with the Father, including the concept of Sonship. As He is God's eternal Word, so He is God's eternal Son (John 1:14). It may also help remove the deep-rooted misunderstandings about this relationship, leading Muslims to understand that Christians believe in only one God, that they do not set up the Son as another God, nor do they displace God by the Son, nor do they make a man into God.

Even among people we depend much on one's word to know what a person wants and does, and what he is like. Through his word a man makes himself known, bringing out what is within him. We trust Abdullah because we trust Abdullah's word. We trust Abdullah's word because we trust Abdullah. We distinguish between Abdullah and his word **and** we equate Abdullah and his word. Both are true.

In a much different, higher and glorious way, the Word which proceeds from God gives expression to God's will and to His acts, and also reveals what He is like in a comprehensible way. Thus the Holy Injil says:

"In the beginning was the Word, and the Word was with God, and the Word was God. He was in the beginning with God; all things were made through him, and without him was not anything made that was made. In him was life, and the life was the light of men . . . . And the Word became flesh and dwelt among us, full of grace and truth; we have beheld his glory, glory as of the only Son from the Father . . . .

No one has ever seen God; the only Son, who is in the bosom[1] of the Father, he has made him known."[2] (RSV, John 1:1-4,14,18)

"This is my **Son**, whom I love. **Listen** to him" (Mark 9:7)

". . . in these last days he has **spoken** to us by his **Son**." (Hebrews 1:2)

[1.] i.e., so intimately is He related to the Father. Should one recall that both the Qur'an and the Bible speak of "the hand of God", "the face of God", etc.?

[2.] "He has made Him known": literally, from the original Greek language of the Holy Injil, "He has exegised (interpreted, explained) Him". It is as if God had revealed His concealed heart through His enfleshed Word.

If a Muslim can accept that the Word of God, which is eternal as God Himself is eternal, can enter into the limitations of time and space and become available in book form, could he not also comprehend that this same Word might be made manifest as a human being? If **on earth** the uncreated Word of God in its created form of a book can be described as both uncreated and created, then cannot the uncreated Word of God in its created form of a human being be described as both uncreated and created, if the one God should so will it? That God has so willed is the testimony of the Holy Injil: God's eternal self-expression, His Word, His Son, has entered human form as Jesus the Messiah.

Jesus as the Son of God: God's Self-Revelation on Earth

We all know that God is the creator of all creation. We know that he continually points mankind to manifold signs in creation and in history which, in turn, point mankind beyond these signs to God Most High Himself as mankind's creator and judge. We know that periodically He has intervened in creation's history through prophets and apostles and the Scriptures. He has mediated through them, whereby He has offered mankind a pattern for life. Probably we all also agree that he bears witness to Himself through human conscience.

In all these ways God reveals to us something about Himself so that we can know something about Him. But does He reveal Himself? Can we know Him?

The response to these crucial questions is found in the astounding claims of Jesus:

"All things have been committed to me by my Father. No one knows the Son except the Father, and no one knows the Father except the Son and those to whom the Son chooses to reveal him." (Matthew 11 :27)

"Don't you know me, Philip, even after I have been among you such a long time? Anyone who has seen me has seen the Father. How can you say, 'Show us the Father'? Don't you believe that I am in the Father, and that the Father is in me?" (John 14:9,10)

Angels, persons and things can reveal to us something about God. But God alone can reveal God! It takes God to reveal Himself to mankind. It takes God to reveal Himself to mankind under created circumstances congenial to human understanding. What better way for the eternal revealer to be revealed to mankind on earth than by clothing His self-expression in human flesh!

In Jesus, His eternal Son, the revealer becomes also the revealed for us. This is why the Holy Bible speaks of Jesus as God manifested in the flesh. In turn, the revealed Son becomes the revealer of the Father among mankind. "Trust in God; trust also in me," says Jesus (John 14:1). In inviting His hearers to trust Him, Jesus is not subtly deflecting trust away from God; rather He is simply affirming that God, forever Most High, is revealing Himself through Jesus by His presence in Jesus.

God, the revealer and the revealed. We would agree that God creates the world, appoints prophets, sends Scriptures and provides laws for human guidance. But can He Himself enter His own creation to be with us? Would this not be unworthy of Him? Would He not demean Himself thereby? Would not His entry into the world conflict with His sovereignty, cloud the brightness of His glory, and make Him less than greater?

God indeed is greater. To Him alone belong the kingdom, the power, and the glory. He alone is sovereign. But, we may ask, what is the nature of God's sovereignty? And how does God Himself manifest the nature of His sovereignty so that humanity too can begin to understand the nature of His sovereignty? Stated otherwise, are we to understand God's sovereignty simply as the sovereignty of any earthly potentate magnified to its ultimate degree? Does God Himself manifest His sovereignty over His creation by remaining aloof from it? Does He safeguard His sovereignty by insulating Himself in celestial serenity, far removed from the suffering and sin of this dying world? Or is it possible that our understanding of God's sovereignty conflicts with His own understanding of His sovereignty; that His thoughts are not our thoughts and our ways are not His ways, even as God has declared through His prophet Isaiah (Isaiah 55:8)? Is it possible that God not only answers but even anticipates the yearning of this prophet: "Oh, that You would rend the heavens and come down . . . !"? (Isaiah 64:1)

According to the Bible, God is love. In Biblical perspective, by entering into this world, God does not demean Himself; rather He exalts Himself. By His visitation on earth, He does not cloud His glory; rather, He magnifies it among mankind. By His presence among us, He does not become the lesser; rather, He becomes the greater for our greater praise. By being not only above us but with us in Jesus Immanuel, He not only acts in conformity with Himself; even more, He is being Himself and He is being what He will be.

Finally, let us briefly summarize the Biblical meaning of Jesus as the Son of God, bearing in mind that 1. "the Lord our God, the Lord is one" (Deuteronomy 6:4) and 2. the Holy Injil itself must be read to grasp the fuller meaning of Jesus' Sonship through His servanthood:

1. The unique Son of God **is of the Father eternally**; by Him God created and sustains the universe. As God's self-expression He is truly God.

2. Because God loved us, the unique Son of God **entered time and space, was born of the Virgin Mary** and was called Jesus the Messiah. As God's self-expression on earth in the form of man He is also truly human.

3. The Son **shares the attributes of the Father**; He is like Him in powerful works and loving self-giving.

4. The Son has been **sent by/from the Father** as His representative to carry out His work of revelation and salvation.

5. The Son is the Father's **personal message**, God expressing Himself and His love in a way that can be seen and heard and comprehended by humanity.

6. The Son **serves the Father** perfectly; the Father is also responsive to the will of the Son.

7. The Father and the Son are **One** in a unique relationship of complete mutuality between Master and Servant, sending One and sent One, revealed One and revealing One.

8. Those who believe in the unique Servant/Son sent by God, God's personal Good News" ("Evangel" or "Injil"), and who follow Him, can become His "brothers and "sisters"; they can become adopted, obedient children of God.

Praise and glory and wisdom and thanks
and honour and power and strength
be to our God forever and ever.
Amen!
(Revelation 7:12)"

SUMMARY HIGHLIGHTS

There is so much that can be said from a very humble and healthy perspective concerning both the Bible and the Quran. From a spiritual concept, I am convinced that there are passages in the Quran that applied very explicitly for the Prophet Muhammad's time frame. Looking intensely at the period of time, it is most obvious how He was successful in that commission. As I write these words, I know many will find fault with that statement.

Looking at the Bible, most would agree it is not all inclusive and complete in all aspects of GOD. That being said, it should be easy to consider the Bible as being Basic Instructions Before Leaving Earth. Have reproductions of the Quran given way to altered and twisted messages as given to the Prophet Muhammad? It appears to be a very obvious, YES. I stated before, Truth will enforce itself. The Quran is overflowing with so much Truth, as is the Bible. Each individual has a responsibility to themselves, their family, their community, state and country to know and be filled with Truth. As we are told to love and pray for our enemies, cloth and feed them; we should have learned that all life is precious and from GOD. So who gave us permission to intercede as Judges for GOD, in carrying out the executions of mass populations? Neither the Bible or the Quran supports such actions and thoughts. We must strive to know GOD as we study the Word of GOD. We must be willing first and foremost to shed our swelling image of self, so that we may be able to receive our daily bread (Word of GOD). It is also so very important to realize the spiritual depth of GOD's Word in the Bible and GOD's Word in the Quran.

Political greed for power will continue to grow, spread, and manifest itself in all forms of deception and motive. If we feel and realize that our own Government is corrupt and dangerous to the health of our Nation, we must first realize that we voted for those people in that Government (whether by willful vote or absence of willful vote). If we don't agree with the policies and motives of our Government, then we must put a better quality of leaders in that Government. In our Democracy as it is, we as citizens have the power and authority to repeal by majority vote any law or program, our politicians may enact. We can tell them "YES" or "NO". Until we have done that, we as individuals are commissioned to obey the policies of the Government in power.

As citizens of our country, we should continually strive to seek the truth. This applies to citizens of every country. This is the greatest way to know the difference between prejudiced propaganda and the Light of Truth. Both the Bible and the Quran are strong foundations for such discernment. Let us all discipline ourselves to think past the nose on our face before we speak, mean what we are about to say (if we must speak), and say what we mean. There is so much power in both vain spoken words and well-chosen words.

POWER OF WORDS

The abuse, misuse, and demeaning value of words in developed societies is appalling. This atrocity appears most apparent in the U.S. Just as many gifted individuals are gifted with profiling dangerous and murdering criminals, I am gifted with profiling parents after observing children for only a few minutes. I can determine the mentality, aptitude, attitude, maturity level, parental skill level of the parents of all children. Often times I can identify an only child of a family. Let me share with you two examples of what I am referring to. The first example will be of a young brother and sister, of approximately four years of age. They will be playing with a number of children their approximate same age. As we watch the children playing we notice the sister of the two look towards her parent, then get up and walk over to her parent. We observe the parent saying something to the girl and then she hurries off towards her brother and says something to him and then runs over to the children she was playing with. We observe some words being spoken among the children and then we observe both the brother and sister joining each other, joining hands, and walking towards their parents. As they gather together with their parents, they all pick up a few personal items and head off towards the family car.

In the second example, we observe a parent sitting on a bench, constantly yelling commands to one child. We hear such commands as "Don't get dirty", "Stop taking his toys, those are not yours", "DO NOT climb up that slide". We immediately see the child continue climbing and the parent rise and rush over to the child and grab him/her off the ladder leading up to the top of a slide. Over the excited chatter of all the children, we hear the parent telling the child: "If you don't listen to me, we are going home, ok?"

In the first example, we saw two children enjoying themselves with their group of friends. We never hear the voice of the parents. When it was time to leave the playground, the family did so without incident. In the second example, the peacefulness and joy of the playground was bombarded with an endless stream of commands from the parent(s). Following this insane display of control, the parent asked for the child's approval (—"we are going home, ok?"). I try to imagine what the parent would have done, had the child said, "NO" (when asked if it was ok to immediately pack up and go home)? Why do parents of today seek the approval of their children? When parents allow their children to dictate to them for the first ten years of their lives, why are they so traumatized when the child continues to dictate to the parents for the next twenty years? It is very clear that in the first scenario, words of the parent(s) had strong meaning and value. In the second scenario, the parent over used words and the child ignored most of what the parent said. Those spoken words had little value.

Perhaps in day to day living, so many people never learned the specific meaning of words. An example of this would be a husband and wife sitting in their living room. The wife is engrossed in a television movie and the husband is watching a large placo swimming about and feeding in a nearby fish aquarium. The husband comments that the placo needs to be in a larger tank. The wife informs the husband that if some of the scenic decorations in the tank were removed, the placo would have more room. The husband is not only stunned at his wife's comment but is wary that she has just opened the door for a heated discussion. I ask you the reader: "How does making more room in the fish tank change the overall dimensions of the tank, to make it larger"? The very obvious fact of the matter is—it doesn't. If the original lateral dimensions of the aquarium were 48 inches by 20 inches, taking everything out of the tank would not make the tank enlarge to 60 inches by 24 inches.

In reality, do people not know and understand the meaning of words? Could it be that these same people just don't respect the speaker of words? In any case, it is a very sad dilemma.

Let us consider the power of words. When people speak hurtful and slanderous things about someone, those words cause damage that can never be taken back. I was told a story by an elder friend once. He asked me: If you were to climb a high steeple on a windy day, with a sack full of feathers and you were to shake those feathers into the wind, could you possibly find and retrieve every feather? Of course, I replied: "no I could not". He told me, it is the same with words we speak. Once they are spoken, they can never be unspoken. He impressed upon me how very important it is to: (1) take a moment to think about what I want to say, (2) think about how to say what I want to convey, (3) be articulate about what I speak, and (4) be certain I mean what I speak.

How often have we heard the following statements from our friends or others?

> "I was just talking to pass the time. I didn't really mean anything I said."
> "I didn't know you were serious."
> "I thought you were joking"
> "He/She didn't really mean anything by what he/she said."
> "He/She was just venting."

Words have POWER. Spoken words can put a smile on a person's face. Spoken words can lift a person out of depression. Words can save a life or words can destroy a life. The Bible teaches us that Words lifted Lazarus up from a grave. Words raised up mighty mountains from the earth. Words caused a bush to shrivel and die. Words sent a multitude of angels out of Heaven to never return. Words healed the sick and ill. Words gave sight to the blind. Words calmed a raging storm. Words sent a legion of demons into a herd of swine. Words sent pestilence and death to a Kingdom giving birth to the Passover. Words parted the Red Sea. It was a Word(s) that caused 40 days and

40 nights of torrential rain, flooding the earth to destroy all that was evil in mankind. **<u>Words Do Have Power!</u>**

All the facts, questions, discussions, deceptions, and revelations bring us to a most important question; "What was/is JESUS"? Throughout the Christian world, He is known and accepted by all the names of GOD. What is the mystery revolving around Him? Why did he give us an example of how to pray, which we adopted as the "Lord's Prayer"? What do the words of the "Lord's Prayer" mean? What do the Words of so many Hymns and songs of Praise mean? Do we Christians stand in our own private self-righteous shadows, speaking and singing recited words or do we truly feel the conviction of their deep true meaning? What power do these words hold?

WHAT IS JESUS? The truth of this matter is revealed in the Bible Book of John: "In the beginning was the Word, and the Word was with God, and the Word was God"(John 1:1 KJ). "And the Word was made flesh, and dwelt among us, (and we beheld his glory, the glory as of the only begotten of the Father,) full of grace and truth" (John 1:6 KJ). In the person of Jesus, man and history witnessed the Power of the WORD. Of so many things, the person of Jesus was Truth, Knowledge, Wisdom and Power. Let us also consider His Words: "For where two or three are gathered together in my name, there am I in the midst of them" (Mathew 18:20 KJ). Try to imagine the depth of what He revealed in this statement. Where two or more are gathered together in (Truth, Knowledge, and Wisdom), there I am in the midst of them (Power). Where two or more are gathered together in the Truth of the WORD, the Knowledge of the WORD, and the Wisdom of the WORD, there shall I be also. The Bible tells us that Jesus is the **WORD.** It is also written that He is **TRUTH**. I offer for your deepest consideration that a combined measure of these things: Truth, Knowledge, and Wisdom will produce a relationship spirit that will grow in unimaginable strength and will see a most gloriously lightened pathway to the throne of GOD. This applies to all societies of this world, be they called Christian, Muslim, Jew, Catholics, Baptists, Lutherans, English, French, Russian, etc.

I submit the following words for your deepest consideration, also. If we believe and breathe, in GOD and (His)WORD, which is and of GOD according to what we are given, what is there to war about, among ourselves? What is the meaning of a word? What does the WORD mean? Do we speak what we mean? Do we mean what we speak?

> ""He (God) has sent down to you the Book (the Qur'an) with truth, confirming what was revealed before; And He sent down the Torah (of Moses) and the Gospel (of Jesus) before this as a guide in humankind; and He sent down the Criterion (the Qur'an)." (Qur'an 3:3-4)" taken from http://www.discoverislam.com/poster.asp?poster=DIP2004_11&page=1 20 May 2013

What "IF" all GOD focused and GOD centered people of the world could be more practiced in a good, unselfish, and compassionate life standard? What "IF" all GOD believing people of the world focused on preventing faith based persecution and committed themselves to being vessels of GOD's light and will towards humankind? What "IF" all GOD centered people joined together in using the weapons of prayer given to us, to have and to hold dominion over all things (evil) of the world, as we were given and are commissioned to exercise? What "IF" we truly believed in the power of words?

What does Muslim mean?

What does Christian mean?

Perhaps the Bible is the greatest source to illustrate that words are either "*blessings*" or "*curses*" upon the ears which they fall. What do you speak? What ears hear your words?

REFERENCES

(Bucaille 1994, 127) Taken from SNAKES FROM STAVES? SCIENCE, SCRIPTURES, AND THE SUPERNATURAL IN MAURICE BUCAILLE by Stefano Bigliard

Tacitus, The Annals of Imperial Rome, Penguin Books, c. 1965, reprint ed.1966, p. 354.

Maya Angelou http://www.goodreads.com/author/quotes/3503.Maya_Angelou?page=2 taken 03 June 2013

Red Sea Crossing (Ron Wyatt's Research on the Exodus to the Red Sea), Arc Discovery International, Taken from http://www.arkdiscovery.com/red_sea_crossing.htm 15 May 2013

Historic Timeline, BC; Taken from http://www.fincher.org/History/WorldBC.shtml 14 May 2013

BBC.CO.UK, BBC Religions taken from http://www.bbc.co.uk/religion/religions/ 15 May 2012

CE—Common Era, Used in the place of A.D./AD, (After Christ) http://www.biblewise.com/archives/2005/november/overview/questions.htm

Christian Denominations List (Brief) http://www.netministries.org/denomlst.htm

Hartford Institute http://hirr.hartsem.edu/denom/homepages.html

List of "ism" words taken from http://www.morewords.com/contains/ism/ 15 May 2013

Early youth marriages taken from http://www.myjewishlearning.com/life/Relationships/Spouses_and_Partners/About_Marriage/Ancient_Jewish_Marriage.shtml 15 May 2013

Bible Facts, Bible Society In Israel taken from http://www.biblesocietyinisrael.com/index.php?option=com_content&view=article&id=58&Itemid=53 15 May 2013

Names of GOD1 (900 names) http://christiananswers.net/dictionary/namesofgod.html

Hebrew Names of GOD http://www.hebrew4christians.com/Names_of_G-d/El/el.html

Lilly of the Valley, Names of GOD http://www.lillyofthevalleyva.com/jesuslovesyou-godsnames-complist.html

99 Names of Allah http://www.4islam.com/99Names.shtml

Hagarites, I Chronicles 5:10,19,20 and Psalm 83:6. The account in I Chronicles 5:10, Dr. C. I. Scofield (Notes in the *New Scofield Reference Bible*, Oxford University Press, 1967)

Muslim, Origin of *MUSLIM;* Arabic *Muslim,* literally, one who submits (to GOD) First Known Use: circa 1615

A Short Biography of Prophet Muhammad January 29, 2004 http://www.quranicstudies.com/prophet-muhammad/a-short-biography-of-prophet-muhammad/

(2005, 12). Power of Words. *StudyMode.com*. Retrieved 12, 2005, from http://www.studymode.com/essays/Power-Words-75759.html

The Power of Words. (2008, February 01). In WriteWork.com. Retrieved May 20, 2013, from http://www.writework.com/essay/power-words

KJ Bible Standard King James Version (Pure Cambridge)

The Independent, dated Saturday 11 March 2006, taken from http://www.independent.co.uk/news/science/how-islamic-inventors-changed-the-world-469452.html 02 June 2013)

Similarities between Islam, Christianity and Judaism—Video Lecture by Dr. Zakir Naik

http://www.institutealislam.com/similarities-between-islam-christianity-and-judaism-video-lecture-by-dr-zakir-naik/

Books by Ernest Hahn
More on Who is Jesus?
Answering Islam Home Page

APPENDIX A

THE NAMES OF GOD
OLD TESTAMENT NAMES FOR GOD

ELOHIM   Genesis 1:1, Psalm 19:1 meaning
                             "God", a reference to God's power and
                             might.

ADONAI   Malachi 1:6 meaning "Lord", a
                             reference to the Lordship of God.

JEHOVAH—YAHWEH   Genesis 2:4 a reference to God's divine
                             salvation.

JEHOVAH-MACCADDESHEM   Exodus 31:13 meaning "The Lord thy
                             sanctifier"

JEHOVAH-ROHI   Psalm 23:1 meaning "The Lord my
                             shepherd"

JEHOVAH-SHAMMAH   Ezekiel 48:35 meaning "The Lord who
                             is present"

JEHOVAH-RAPHA   Exodus 15:26 meaning "The Lord our
                             healer"

JEHOVAH-TSIDKENU   Jeremiah 23:6 meaning "The Lord our
                             Righteousness"

JEHOVAH-JIREH   Genesis 22:13-14 meaning "The Lord
                             will provide"

JEHOVAH-NISSI   Exodus 17:15 meaning "The Lord our
                             banner"

JEHOVAH-SHALOM   Judges 6:24 meaning "The Lord is
                             peace"

JEHOVAH-SABBAOTH   Isaiah 6:1-3 meaning "The Lord of
                             Hosts"

JEHOVAH-GMOLAH	Jeremiah 51:6 meaning "The God of Recompense"
EL-ELYON	Genesis 14:17-20, Isaiah 14:13-14 meaning "The most high God
EL-ROI	Genesis 16:13 meaning "The strong one who sees"
EL-SHADDAI	Genesis 17:1, Psalm 91:1 meaning "The God of the mountains or God Almighty"
EL-OLAM	Isaiah 40:28-31 meaning "The everlasting God"

MORE NAMES OF GOD
Father, Son, Holy Spirit

• AVENGER	1Thess.4:6
• ABBA	Romans 8:15
• ADVOCATE	I John 2:1 (kjv)
• ALMIGHTY	Genesis 17:1
• ALL IN ALL	Colossians 3:11
• ALPHA	Revelation 22:13
• AMEN	Revelation 3:14
• ANCIENT OF DAYS	Daniel 7:9
• ANOINTED ONE	Psalm 2:2
• APOSTLE	Hebrews 3:1
• ARM OF THE LORD	Isaiah 53:1
• AUTHOR OF ETERNAL SALVATION	Hebrews 5:9
• AUTHOR OF OUR FAITH	Hebrews 12:2
• AUTHOR OF PEACE	1 Cor. 14:33

• BEGINNING	Revelation 21:6
• BISHOP OF SOULS	1 Peter 2:25
• BLESSED & HOLY RULER	1 Timothy 6:15
• BRANCH	Jeremiah 33:15
• BREAD OF GOD	John 6:33
• BREAD OF LIFE	John 6:35
• BREATH OF LIFE	Genesis 2:7, Revelation 11:11
• BRIDEGROOM	Isaiah 62:5
• BRIGHT MORNING STAR	Revelation 22:16
• BUCKLER	2 Sam.22:31kjv, Psalm 18:2kjv, Psalm 18:30kjv, Proverbs 2:7kjv

- CAPTAIN OF SALVATION   Hebrews 2:10
- CARPENTER   Mark 6:3
- CHIEF SHEPHERD   1 Peter 5:4
- CHOSEN ONE   Isaiah 42:1
- CHRIST   Matthew 22:42
- CHRIST OF GOD   Luke 9:20
- CHRIST THE LORD   Luke 2:11
- CHRIST, SON OF LIVING GOD   Matthew 16:16
- COMFORTER   John 14:26(kjv)
- COMMANDER   Isaiah 55:4
- CONSOLATION OF ISRAEL   Luke 2:25
- CONSUMING FIRE   Deut. 4:24, Heb. 12:29
- CORNERSTONE   Isaiah 28:16
- COUNSELOR   Isaiah 9:6
- CREATOR   1 Peter 4:19
- CROWN OF BEAUTY   Isaiah 28:5

- DAYSPRING   Luke 1:78
- DELIVERER   Romans 11:26
- DESIRED OF ALL NATIONS   Haggai 2:7
- DIADEM OF BEAUTY   Isaiah 28:5
- DOOR   John 10:7(kjv)
- DWELLING PLACE   Psalm 90:1

- ELECT ONE   Isaiah 42:1
- EMMANUEL   Matthew 1:23(kjv)
- END   Revelation 21:6
- ETERNAL GOD   Deut. 33:27
- ETERNAL LIFE   1 John 5:20
- ETERNAL SPIRIT   Hebrews 9:14
- EVERLASTING FATHER   Isaiah 9:6

• EVERLASTING GOD   <u>Genesis 21:33</u>
• EXCELLENT   <u>Psalm 148:13(kjv)</u>

• FAITHFUL & TRUE   <u>Revelation 19:11</u>
• FAITHFUL WITNESS   <u>Revelation 1:5</u>
• FATHER   <u>Matthew 6:9</u>
• FIRSTBORN   <u>Rom.8:29</u>, <u>Rev.1:5</u>, <u>Col.1:15</u>
• FIRSTFRUITS   <u>1 Cor.15:20-23</u>
• FORTRESS   <u>Jeremiah 16:19</u>
• FOUNDATION   <u>1 Cor. 3:11</u>
• FOUNTAIN OF LIVING WATERS   <u>Jeremiah 2:13</u>
• FRIEND   <u>Matthew 11:19</u>
• FULLERS' SOAP   <u>Malachi 3:2(kjv)</u>

• GENTLE WHISPER   <u>1 Kings 19:12</u>
• GIFT OF GOD   <u>John 4:10</u>
• GLORY OF THE LORD   <u>Isaiah 40:5</u>
• GOD   <u>Genesis 1:1</u>
• GOD ALMIGHTY   <u>Genesis 17:1</u>
• GOD OF THE WHOLE EARTH   <u>Isaiah 54:5</u>
• GOD OVER ALL   <u>Romans 9:5</u>
• GOD WHO SEES ME   <u>Genesis 16:13</u>
• GOODNESS   <u>Psalm 144:2(kjv)</u>
• GOOD SHEPHERD   <u>John 10:11</u>
• GOVERNOR   <u>Psalm 22:28(kjv)</u>
• GREAT HIGH PRIEST   <u>Hebrews 4:14</u>
• GREAT SHEPHERD   <u>Hebrews 13:20</u>
• GUIDE   <u>Psalm 48:14</u>

- HEAD OF THE BODY   Colossians 1:18
- HEAD OF THE CHURCH   Ephesians 5:23
- HEIR OF ALL THINGS   Hebrews 1:2
- HIDING PLACE   Psalm 32:7
- HIGHEST   Luke 1:76
- HIGH PRIEST   Hebrews 3:1
- HIGH PRIEST FOREVER   Hebrews 6:20
- HOLY GHOST   John 14:26
- HOLY ONE   Acts 2:27
- HOLY ONE OF ISRAEL   Isaiah 49:7
- HOLY SPIRIT   John 15:26
- HOPE   Titus 2:13
- HORN OF SALVATION   Luke 1:69
- HUSBAND   Isaiah 54:5, Jere.31:32, Hosea 2:16

- I AM   Exodus 3:14, John 8:58
- IMAGE OF GOD   2 Cor. 4:4
- IMAGE OF HIS PERSON   Hebrews 1:3 (kjv)
- IMMANUEL   Isaiah 7:14
- INTERCESSOR   Romans 8:26,27,34 Hebrews 7:25

- JAH   Psalm 68:4(kjv)
- JEALOUS   Exodus 34:14(kjv)
- JEHOVAH   Psalm 83:18(kjv)
- JESUS   Matthew 1:21
- JESUS CHRIST OUR LORD   Romans 6:23
- JUDGE   Isaiah 33:22, Acts 10:42
- JUST ONE   Acts 22:14

• KEEPER	Psalm 121:5
• KING	Zechariah 9:9
• KING ETERNAL	1 Timothy 1:17
• KING OF GLORY	Psalm 24:10
• KING OF JEWS	Matthew 27:11
• KING OF KINGS	1 Timothy 6:15
• KING OF SAINTS	Revelation 15:3

• LAMB OF GOD	John 1:29
• LAST ADAM	1 Cor. 15:45
• LAWGIVER	Isaiah 33:22
• LEADER	Isaiah 55:4
• LIFE	John 14:6
• LIGHT OF THE WORLD	.John 8:12
• LIKE AN EAGLE	Deut. 32:11
• LILY OF THE VALLEYS	Song 2:1
• LION OF THE TRIBE OF JUDAH	Revelation 5:5
• LIVING GOD	Daniel 6:20
• LIVING STONE	1 Peter 2:4
• LIVING WATER	John 4:10
• LORD	John 13:13
• LORD GOD ALMIGHTY	Revelation 15:3
• LORD JESUS CHRIST	1 Cor. 15:57
• LORD OF ALL	Acts 10:36
• LORD OF GLORY	1 Cor. 2:8
• LORD OF HARVEST	Matthew 9:38
• LORD OF HOSTS	Haggai 1:5
• LORD OF LORDS	1 Tim. 6:15
• LORD OUR RIGHTEOUSNESS	Jeremiah 23:6
• LOVE	1 John 4:8
• LOVING KINDNESS	Psalm 144:2

- MAKER   Job 35:10, Psalm 95:6
- MAJESTY ON HIGH   Hebrews 1:3
- MAN OF SORROWS   Isaiah 53:3
- MASTER   Luke 5:5
- MEDIATOR   1 Timothy 2:5
- MERCIFUL GOD   Jeremiah 3:12
- MESSENGER OF THE   Malachi 3:1
  COVENANT
- MESSIAH   John 4:25
- MIGHTY GOD   Isaiah 9:6
- MIGHTY ONE   Isaiah 60:16
- MOST UPRIGHT   Isaiah 26:7

- NAZARENE   Matthew 2:23

- OFFSPRING OF DAVID   Revelation 22:16
- OMEGA   Revelation 22:13
- ONLY BEGOTTEN SON   John 1:18(kjv)
- OUR PASSOVER LAMB   1 Cor. 5:7
- OUR PEACE   Ephesians 2:14

- PHYSICIAN   Luke 4:23
- PORTION   Psalm 73:26, Psalm 119:57
- POTENTATE   1 Timothy 6:15
- POTTER   Isaiah 64:8
- POWER OF GOD   1 Cor. 1:24
- PRINCE OF LIFE   Acts 3:15
- PRINCE OF PEACE   Isaiah 9:6
- PROPHET   Acts 3:22

- PROPHET OF THE HIGHEST   Luke 1:76
- PROPITIATION   1John 2:2, 1John 4:10
- PURIFIER   Malachi 3:3

- QUICKENING SPIRIT   1 Corinthians 15:45(kjv)

- RABBONI (TEACHER)   John 20:16
- RADIANCE OF GOD'S GLORY   Heb.1:3
- REDEEMER   Job 19:25
- REFINER'S FIRE   Malachi 3:2
- REFUGE   Jeremiah 16:19
- RESURRECTION   John 11:25
- REWARDER   Hebrews 11:6
- RIGHTEOUS ONE   1 John 2:1
- ROCK   1 Cor.10:4
- ROOT OF DAVID   Rev. 22:16
- ROSE OF SHARON   Song 2:1
- RULER OF GOD'S CREATION   Rev. 3:14
- RULER OVER KINGS OF EARTH   Rev 1:5
- RULER OVER ISRAEL   Micah 5:2

- SAVIOR   Luke 2:11
- SCEPTRE   Numbers 24:17
- SEED   Genesis 3:15
- SERVANT   Isaiah 42:1
- SHADE   Psalm 121:5
- SHEPHERD OF OUR SOULS   1Peter 2:25
- SHIELD   Genesis 15:1

- SHILOH   Genesis 49:10
- SONG   Exodus 15:2, Isaiah 12:2
- SON OF DAVID   Matthew 1:1
- SON OF GOD   Matthew 27:54
- SON OF MAN   Matthew 8:20
- SON OF THE MOST HIGH   Luke 1:32
- SOURCE   Hebrews 5:9
- SPIRIT   John 4:24
- SPIRIT OF ADOPTION   Romans 8:15
- SPIRIT OF GOD   Genesis 1:2
- SPIRIT OF TRUTH   John 14:17, 15:26, 16:13
- STAR OUT OF JACOB   Numbers 24:17
- STRENGTH   Jeremiah 16:19
- STONE   1 Peter 2:8
- STONE OF ISRAEL   Genesis 49:24
- STRONGHOLD   Nahum 1:7
- STRONG TOWER   Proverbs 18:10
- SUN OF RIGHTEOUSNESS   Malachi 4:2

- TEACHER   John 13:13
- TEMPLE   Revelation 21:22
- THE ONE   Psalm 144:2,10
- TRUE LIGHT   John 1:9
- TRUE WITNESS   Revelation 3:14
- TRUTH   John 14:6

- VINE   John 15:5

• WALL OF FIRE	Zechariah 2:5
• WAY	John 14:6
• WISDOM OF GOD	1 Cor. 1:24
• WONDERFUL	Isaiah 9:6
• WORD	John 1:1
• WORD OF GOD	Revelation 19:13

• YAH	Isaiah 12:2(kjv), Psalm 68:4(nkjv)

APPENDIX B

The Names of GOD in Islam

1. **Allah (The Name of Allah)** Allah is Allah's name only. Nothing else can assume this name or share it.

2. **Ar-Rahmaan (The Compassionate)** He is the one who wills mercy and good for all creation at all times. He pours upon all creation infinite bounties.

3. **Ar-Raheem (The Most Merciful)** He is the source of infinite mercy and beneficence, who rewards with eternal gifts the one who uses His bounties for the good.

4. **Al-Malik (The Sovereign)** He is the owner and rule of the entire universe, visible and invisible, and of all creation, from before the beginning and after the end.

5. **Al-Quddoos (The Most Holy)** He is the most pure one, devoid of all blemish, shortcoming, weakness, heedlessness and error.

6. **As-Salaam (The Bestower of Peace)** He is the one who saves the believing servants from all dangers, bringing them peace, blessings and security of paradise.

7. **Al-Mu'min (The Granter of Security)** He is the illuminator of the light of faith in hearts. He is the comforter, the protector of the ones who take refuge in Him.

8. Al-Muhaymin (The Protector) He is the protector and the guardian. He is the one who sees to the growth of His creation, leading them where they are destined to go.

9. Al-'Azeez (The Mighty) He is the victorious one whom no force can overwhelm. There is no strength in this universe that can stand before His will.

10. Al-Jabbaar (The Compeller) He is the repairer of the broken, the completer of the lacking, the one who can enforce His will without any opposition.

11. Al-Mutakabbir (The Majestic) He is the greatest, who shows His greatness in everything, on all occasions.

12. Al-Khaaliq (The Creator) He is the one who creates from nothing, creating at the same time the states, conditions and sustenance of all that He has created. He establishes how, when and where creation will take place.

13. Al-Baari' (The Maker) He is the one who orders His creation with perfect harmony—not only each thing within itself, but everything in accordance with everything else.

14. Al-Musawwir (The Fashioner of Forms) He is the one who, without using any model, shapes everything in the most perfect manner.

15. Al-Ghaffaar (The Forgiver) He is the one who accepts repentance and forgives.

16. Al-Qahhaar (The Subduer) He is the ever-dominating one, who has surrounded all His creation from without and within with His irresistible power. Nothing can escape Him.

17. Al-Wahhaab (The Bestower) He is the donor of all, without conditions, without limits, without asking any benefits or return, giving everything to everyone, everywhere, always.

18. Ar-Razzaaq (The Provider) He is the sustainer. Sustenance, both spiritual and physical, is needed to maintain the creation

19. Al-Fattaah (The Opener) He is the opener and the solver, the easer of all that is locked, tied and hardened.

20. Al-'Aleem (The All-Knowing) He is the one who knows all. He knows what has happened, what is happening and what will happen from the beginning to the end.

21. Al-Qaabidh (The Withholder) He is the one who constricts. All existence is in His power. The life on this planet is a test for us, but He does not test His servants above their ability.

22. Al-Baasit (The Expander) He is the one who releases abundance, joy, relief and ease after difficulties.

23. Al-Khaafidh (The Abaser) He is the one who raises His creatures to honor and fame and who can cast them down to be the lowest of the low.

24. Ar-Raafi' (The Exalter) He is the one who raises His creatures to honor and fame and who can cast them down to be the lowest of the low.

25. Al-Mu'iz (The Bestower of Honor) He is the one who honors and the one humiliates.

26. Al-Muthil (The Humiliator) He is the one who honors and the one humiliates.

27. As-Samee' (The All-Hearing) He is the one who hears all—that which comes from the lips, passes through the minds, is felt by the hearts, the rustling of the leaves in the wind, the footsteps of ants and the atoms moving through the void.

28. Al-Baseer (The All-Seeing) He is the one who sees all—that which has passed, all there is and all there will be until the end of time.

29. Al-Hakam (The Judge) He is the one who orders. He is the bringer of justice and truth. He judges and executes His justice.

30. Al-'Adl (The Just) He is the absolute justice. Justice secures peace, balance, order and harmony. He is the enemy of tyrants.

31. Al-Lateef (The Most Affectionate, The Knower of Subtleties) He is the most delicate, fine, gentle and beautiful one. He is the one who knows the finest details of beauty.

32. Al-Khabeer (The All-Aware) He is the one who is aware of the hidden inner occurances in everything. He is the one whose cognizance reaches the deepest, darkest, hidden corners of His kingdom, where neither human intelligence nor His angels can penetrate.

33. Al-Haleem (The Forbearing) He is forbearing in the punishment of the guilty. He waits, giving time to the sinner to realize His guilt and ask forgiveness in order that He may forgive him rather than punish him.

34. Al-'Atheem (The Magnificient) He is the greatest on the earth below and in the heavens above, in realms where our sight cannot reach and of which our minds cannot conceive. He is the absolute and perfect greatness.

35. Al-Ghafoor (The Forgiving) He is the most forgiving one. He veils our faults from the eyes of other men, from the angels and relieves us from the suffering of continual remembrance of our faults.

36. Ash-Shakoor (The Grateful) He is the one who repays a good deed with a much greater reward. Thankfulness is to return good with good.

37. Al-'Aliyy (The Highest) He is the highest one. He is higher than the whole of the created universe. His nearness and farness and His being high cannot be measured by the limits of human intellect.

38. Al-Kabeer (The Greatest) He is the greatest, whose greatness stretches from before the beginning until after the end. There is no difference for Him between the creation of an atom and the infinite-seeming universe. This is His grandeur as much as we can understand it. He is greater than that.

39. Al-Hafeeth (The Preserver) He is the one who remembers all that was and all that is, keeping in His divine protection all that there will be.

40. Al-Muqeet (The Sustainer) He is the nourisher of all creation. He creates the nourishment of each of His creature before He creates them. No one can take away the nourishment destined for each element of the creation.

41. Al-Haseeb (The Reckoner) He is the one who takes account of all and everything that His creation does or is subjected to.

42. Al-Jaleel (The Exalted) He is the lord of majesty and might. His might, greatness and eternity bear no resemblance to any energy, matter, or time.

43. Al-Kareem (The Generous) He is the generous one. His greatest generosity is His mercy, through which He forgives when He could punish.

44. Ar-Raqeeb (The Watchful) He is the one who watches everything always. This scrutiny of every detail in the existence of all creation is in part protective.

45. Al-Mujeeb (The Responsive) He is the one who responds to all the needs of His servants. He is closer to His creatures than they are to themselves. He is not any closer to a saint than He is to you or to a mustard seed.

46. Al-Waasi' (The All-Encompassing) He is the limitless vastness, whose knowledge, power, mercy, generosity and all other beautiful attributes are infinite.

47. Al-Hakeem (The Wise) He is perfectly wise in His knowledge and His deeds. There is no doubt or uncertainty in His knowledge, nor does it have an end.

48. Al-Wadood (The Most Loving) He is the one who loves His good servants. He is the only one who is worthy of love.

49. Al-Majeed (The Most Glorious) He is glorious and majestic in the whole of His creation and beyond. No hand reaches Him, no power can touch Him, yet He is closer to His servants than their own souls. His state is pure perfection. His acts are pure wisdom.

50. Al-Baa'ith (The Resurrector) He is the raiser from the dead. He will give life back to all creation on the day of judgment.

51. Ash-Shaheed (The Witness) He is the one who witnesses all that happens everywhere at all times.

52. Al-Haqq (The Truth) He is the truth, whose being is ever unchanged.

53. Al-Wakeel (The Trustee) He is the ultimate and faithful trustee. Men think that they are able to do, but He is the one who does everything. He can replace everything in the universe, but nothing can replace Him nor can stand on its own without depending on Him.

54. Al-Qawiyy (The Most Strong) He is the most strong one, the inexhaustible. He possesses all strength. He can create a billion universes with the same ease with which He creates a blade of grass.

55. Al-Mateen (The Firm) He is perfect in His strength and in His firmness. None can be saved from this strength, no force can oppose it and nothing can weaken it.

56. Al-Waliyy (The Patron) He is the protecting friend of His good servants. He eliminates their difficulties and gives them guidance, peace and success in their affairs in this world and in the hereafter.

57. Al-Hameed (The Praiseworthy) He is the most praiseworthy. All that exists praise Him with their words, their actions or simply by their very existence. He is the only one who is worthy of devotion, respect, thankfulness and praise.

58. Al-Muhsee (The Reckoner) He is the possessor of all quantitative knowledge. He sees and knows everything in its reality. He knows the number of all existence in the universe down to the number of breaths exhaled and inhaled by each of His creatures.

59. Al-Mubdi' (The Originator) He is the originator of all. He creates without model or material.

60. Al-Mu'eed (The Restorer) He is the restorer of things He has created and destroyed.

61. Al-Muhyee (The Giver of Life) He is the giver of life to things without life. He is the one who has created life and death. No one else can do that.

62. Al-Mumeet (The Giver of Death) He is the creator of death. All who are alive will certainly die. Man is made of a combination of the flesh and the soul. The body is temporal, the soul is eternal.

63. Al-Hayy (The Ever-Living) He is the perfectly alive and ever-living one. He is cognizant of all and all actions are His. All this known and will be known is within His knowledge. All existence is always comprehended in His action.

64. Al-Qayyoom (The Self-Subsisting Sustainer of All) He is the ever self-existing one upon whom the existence of all depends. His existence depends on none other than Himself.

65. Al-Waajid (The Finder) He finds and obtains whatever He wishes whenever He wishes. It is even superfluous to use the word 'find' because all is in His presence at all times.

66. Al-Maajid (The Glorious) He is the most glorious, who shows infinite generosity and munificence to those close to Him.

67. Al-Waahid/Al-Ahad (The One) He is one. He has no equal, none like Him, nor any partner in His essence, in His attributes, in His actions, in His orders, or in His beautiful names.

68. As-Samad (The Eternally Besought) He is the satisfier of all needs and all is in need of Him. He is the sole recourse; the only place of support where one may go to rid oneself of all trouble and to receive all that one needs through the blessings of this name.

69. Al-Qaadir (The Omnipotent) He is the all powerful who does what He wills the way He wills. He created the universe by Himself, from nothing, with neither material nor model. He said 'BE' and it became.

70. Al-Muqtadir (The Powerful) He is the one who creates all power and has total control over all power. He bestows power upon things on earth and in heaven, and uses them in accordance with His all pervasive wisdom and will.

71. Al-Muqaddim (The Expediter) He brings forward whomever He wills. He advances the chosen among His creation, bringing some above and ahead of others.

72. Al-Mu'akhkhir (The Delayer) He leaves behind whomever He wills and delays advancement.

73. Al-Awwal (The First) He is the first. There is none like Him. His firstness means that there was none prior to Him. He is self-existent, all comes from Him and He is the cause of all that became.

74. Al-Aakhir (The Last) He is the last. He has no beginning. He has no end. He is eternal. He is the last in the sense that the circle of existence begins and ends with Him.

75. Ath-Thaahir (The Manifest) He is the manifest one. He is hidden from those who seek to see by means of their senses, but He is apparent to those who seek to know Him by the wisdom and reason that He has bestowed upon them.

76. Al-Baatin (The Hidden) He is the hidden one. His existence is both manifest and hidden. To truly know the creator is not possible because the knowledge, the mind, the understanding of the created one is limited.

77. Al-Waalee (The Governer) He is the sole manager and governor of the whole creation.

78. Al-Muta'aalee (The Most Exalted) He is the supreme one. His greatness grows. As He gives from His inexhaustible treasures His riches increase. As the needs of His creation increase, His bounties increase.

79. Al-Barr (The Source of All Goodness) He is the perfect doer of good. All goodness and bounty come from Him. He loves for His servants only good, comfort and ease.

80. At-Tawwaab (The Acceptor of Repentance) He is one who constantly turns man to repentance.

81. Al-Muntaqim (The Avenger) He is the great avenger. He punishes those who persist in revolting, raving in their unconsciousness and egotism, creating disharmony, tyrannizing His servants and His creation.

82. Al-'Afuww (The Pardoner) He is the forgiver, the eliminator of sins. He does not often punish the ones who deny, the ones who revolt. He accepts their recognition of their sins as repentance. He erases their sins.

83. Ar-Ra'oof (The Most Kind) He is all clement. In spite of His ability to see our sins, of His being just, of His being able to punish, the fact that He chooses to forgive proves His infinite mercy and clemency.

84. Maalik-ul-Mulk (The Owner of Sovereignity) He is the eternal owner of His kingdom. He shares neither the ownership, nor the power, government or guardianship of the universe with anyone.

85. Dhul-Jalaali Wal-Ikraam (Majestic and Benevolent) He is the lord of majesty and bounty. There is no perfection that does not belong to Him nor any blessing or honor that comes from other than Him.

86. Al-Muqsit (The Just) He is the one who acts and distributes in justice and fairness. How harmonious and balanced is the creation: all the beauties in heaven and earth, mountains, seas, sunsets, flowers and also the eyes to see.

87. Al-Jaami' (The Gatherer) He is the gatherer of whatever He wishes, wherever He wishes. He has gathered together within this universe spaces, galaxies, stars, planets, seas, plants and animals, things whose nature, size, shape and color are different.

88. Al-Ghaniyy (The Self-Sufficient) He is the rich one who is self-sufficient. His essence and attributes have no relationship to anything else. His existence and perfection depend on no other and He does not need to earn His existence.

89. Al-Mughnee (The Enricher) He is the enricher. He renders whomever He wishes rich and whomever He wishes poor.

90. Al-Maani' (The Preventer of Harm) He is the one who averts harm from His creation.

91. Adh-Dhaar (The Distresser) He is the creator of the harmful and evil as He is the creator of the good and beneficial. He has also taught us to opt for the good and avoid the evil. He has given us the power of discrimination and the will and freedom to choose.

92. An-Naafi' (The Propitious) He is the creator of good. He has created man as the best of His creation and He has bestowed upon him gifts which render him unique and superior to the rest of the creation.

93. An-Noor (The Light) He is the light that is shed upon the whole creation, making it apparent. His light brought existence out of the darkness of non-existence.

94. Al-Haadee (The Guide) He is the one who gives guidance, leading His servants to good, beneficence and the fulfillment of their needs.

95. Al-Badee' (The Originator) He is the originator of the creation, having created it without model or material. He does not need previous knowledge to think, to first investigate, to figure things out. Everything He creates is a wonder since He originated it from nothing.

96. Al-Baaqee (The Everlasting) He is the everlasting one who existence in the future is forever. He has neither beginning nor end. The creation will end and time with it. But He will still exist.

97. Al-Waarith (The Ultimate Inheritor) He is the ultimate inheritor, to whom everything is left after its temporal possessors are gone. It is He who exists after all existence disappears. It is He to whom all existence returns.

98. Ar-Rasheed (The Guide to the Right Path) He is the righteous teacher who ordains righteousness for all creatures. In His wisdom He leads all matters to their finality in a perfect way and order.

99. As-Saboor (The Patient One) He is the most patient one. In His creation as in His actions, in His dealings with His creation, nothing is either bigger or smaller, better or worse, earlier or later than it is determined for it to be.

APPENDIX C

World History Timeline (BC)
http://www.fincher.org/History/WorldBC.shtml

World History Timeline (AD)
http://www.fincher.org/History/WorldAD.shtml

Bible Timeline
http://www.fincher.org/History/Bible.shtml

APPENDIX D

Little Known
Muslim Contributions to the World

From coffee to checks and the three-course meal, the Muslim world has given us many innovations that we take for granted in daily life. Paul Vallely nominates 20 of the most influential—and identifies the men of genius behind them

1 The story goes that an Arab named Khalid was tending his goats in the Kaffa region of southern Ethiopia, when he noticed his animals became livelier after eating a certain berry. He boiled the berries to make the first coffee. Certainly the first record of the drink is of beans exported from Ethiopia to Yemen where Sufis drank it to stay awake all night to pray on special occasions. By the late 15th century it had arrived in Mecca and Turkey from where it made its way to Venice in 1645. It was brought to England in 1650 by a Turk named Pasqua Rosee who opened the first coffee house in Lombard Street in the City of London. The Arabic qahwa became the Turkish kahve then the Italian caffé and then English coffee.

2 The ancient Greeks thought our eyes emitted rays, like a laser, which enabled us to see. The first person to realize that light enters the eye, rather than leaving it, was the 10th-century Muslim mathematician, astronomer and physicist Ibn al-Haitham. He invented the first pin-hole camera after noticing the way light came through a hole in window shutters. The smaller the hole, the better the picture, he worked out, and set up the first Camera Obscura (from the Arab word qamara for a dark or private room). He is also credited with being the first man to shift physics from a philosophical activity to an experimental one.

3 A form of chess was played in ancient India but the game was developed into the form we know today, in Persia. From there it spread westward to Europe—where it was introduced by the Moors in Spain in the 10th century—and eastward as far as Japan. The word rook comes from the Persian rukh, which means chariot.

4 A thousand years before the Wright brothers a Muslim poet, astronomer, musician and engineer named Abbas ibn Firnas made several attempts to construct a flying machine. In 852 he jumped from the minaret of the Grand Mosque in Cordoba using a loose cloak stiffened with wooden struts. He hoped to glide like a bird . . . . He didn't. But the cloak slowed his fall, creating what is thought to be the first parachute, and leaving him with only minor injuries. In 875, at age 70, having perfected a machine of silk and eagles' feathers he tried again, jumping from a mountain. He flew to a significant height and stayed aloft for ten minutes but crashed on landing—concluding, correctly, that it was because he had not given his device a tail so it would stall on landing. Baghdad international airport and a crater on the Moon are named after him.

5 Washing and bathing are religious requirements for Muslims, which is perhaps why they perfected the recipe for soap which we still use today. The ancient Egyptians had soap of a kind, as did the Romans who used it more as a pomade. But it was the Arabs who combined vegetable oils with sodium hydroxide and aromatics such as thyme oil. One of the Crusaders' most striking characteristics, to Arab nostrils, was that they did not wash. Shampoo was introduced to England by a Muslim who opened Mahomed's Indian Vapour Baths on Brighton seafront in 1759 and was appointed Shampooing Surgeon to Kings George IV and William IV.

6 Distillation, the means of separating liquids through differences in their boiling points, was invented around the year 800 by Islam's foremost scientist, Jabir ibn Hayyan, who transformed alchemy into chemistry, inventing many of the basic processes and apparatus still in use today—liquefaction, crystallization, distillation, purification, oxidization, evaporation and filtration. As well as discovering sulpheric and nitric acid, he invented the alembic still, giving the world intense rosewater and other perfumes and alcoholic spirits (although drinking them is haram, or forbidden, in Islam). Ibn Hayyan emphasized systematic experimentation and was the founder of modern chemistry.

7 The crank-shaft is a device which translates rotary into linear motion and is central to much of the machinery in the modern world, not least the internal combustion engine. One of the most important mechanical inventions in the history of humankind, it was created by an ingenious Muslim engineer called al-Jazari to raise water for irrigation. His 1206 Book of Knowledge of Ingenious Mechanical Devices shows he also invented or refined the use of valves and pistons, devised some of the first mechanical clocks driven by water and weights, and was the father of robotics. Among his 50 other inventions was the combination lock.

8 Quilting is a method of sewing or tying two layers of cloth with a layer of insulating material in between. It is not clear whether it was invented in the Muslim world or whether it was imported there from India or China. But it certainly came to the West via the Crusaders. They saw it used by Saracen warriors, who wore straw-filled quilted canvas shirts instead of armor. As well as a form of protection, it proved an effective guard against the chafing of the Crusaders' metal armor and was an effective form of insulation—so much so that it became a cottage industry back home in colder climates such as Britain and Holland.

9 The pointed arch so characteristic of Europe's Gothic cathedrals was an invention borrowed from Islamic architecture. It was much stronger than the rounded arch used by the Romans and Normans, thus allowing the building of bigger, higher, more complex and more grand buildings. Other borrowings from Muslim genius included ribbed vaulting, rose windows and dome-building techniques. Europe's castles were also adapted to copy the Islamic world's—with arrow slits, battlements, a barbican and parapets. Square towers and keeps gave way to more easily defended round ones. Henry V's castle architect was a Muslim.

10 Many modern surgical instruments are of exactly the same design as those devised in the 10th century by a Muslim surgeon called al-Zahrawi. His scalpels, bone saws, forceps, fine scissors for eye surgery and many of the 200 instruments he devised are recognizable to a modern surgeon. It was he who discovered that catgut used for internal stitches dissolves away naturally (a discovery he made when his monkey ate his lute strings) and that it can be also used to make medicine capsules. In the 13th century, another Muslim medic named Ibn Nafis described the circulation of the blood, 300 years before William Harvey discovered it. Muslims doctors also invented an aesthetics of opium and alcohol mixes and developed hollow needles to suck cataracts from eyes in a technique still used today.

11 The windmill was invented in 634 for a Persian caliph and was used to grind corn and draw up water for irrigation. In the vast deserts of Arabia, when the seasonal streams ran dry, the only source of power was the wind which blew steadily from one direction for months. Mills had six or 12 sails covered in fabric or palm leaves. It was 500 years before the first windmill was seen in Europe.

12 The technique of inoculation was not invented by Jenner and Pasteur but was devised in the Muslim world and brought to Europe from Turkey by the wife of the English ambassador to Istanbul in 1724. Children in Turkey were vaccinated with cowpox to fight the deadly smallpox at least 50 years before the West discovered it.

13 The fountain pen was invented for the Sultan of Egypt in 953 after he demanded a pen which would not stain his hands or clothes. It held ink in a reservoir and, as with modern pens, fed ink to the nib by a combination of gravity and capillary action.

14 The system of numbering in use all round the world is probably Indian in origin but the style of the numerals is Arabic and first appears in print in the work of the Muslim mathematicians al-Khwarizmi and al-Kindi around 825. Algebra was named after al-Khwarizmi's book, Al-Jabr wa-al-Muqabilah, much of whose contents are still in use. The work of Muslim math scholars was imported into Europe 300 years later by the Italian mathematician Fibonacci. Algorithms and much of the theory of trigonometry came from the Muslim world. And Al-Kindi's discovery of frequency analysis rendered all the codes of the ancient world soluble and created the basis of modern cryptology.

15 Ali ibn Nafi, known by his nickname of Ziryab (Blackbird) came from Iraq to Cordoba in the 9th century and brought with him the concept of the three-course meal—soup, followed by fish or meat, then fruit and nuts. He also introduced crystal glasses (which had been invented after experiments with rock crystal by Abbas ibn Firnas—see No 4).

16 Carpets were regarded as part of Paradise by medieval Muslims, thanks to their advanced weaving techniques, new tinctures from Islamic chemistry and highly developed sense of pattern and arabesque which were the basis of Islam's non-representational art. In contrast, Europe's floors were distinctly earthly, not to say earthy, until Arabian and Persian carpets were introduced. In England, as Erasmus recorded, floors were "covered in rushes, occasionally renewed, but so imperfectly that the bottom layer is left undisturbed, sometimes for 20 years, harboring expectoration, vomiting, the leakage of dogs and men, ale droppings, scraps of fish, and other abominations not fit to be mentioned". Carpets, unsurprisingly, caught on quickly.

17 The modern check comes from the Arabic saqq, a written vow to pay for goods when they were delivered, to avoid money having to be transported across dangerous terrain. In the 9th century, a Muslim businessman could cash a check in China drawn on his bank in Baghdad.

18 By the 9th century, many Muslim scholars took it for granted that the Earth was a sphere. The proof, said astronomer Ibn Hazm, "is that the Sun is always vertical to a particular spot on Earth". It was 500 years before that realization dawned on Galileo. The calculations of Muslim astronomers were so accurate that in the 9th century they reckoned the Earth's circumference to be 40,253.4km—less than 200km out. The scholar al-Idrisi took a globe depicting the world to the court of King Roger of Sicily in 1139.

19 Though the Chinese invented saltpeter gunpowder, and used it in their fireworks, it was the Arabs who worked out that it could be purified using potassium nitrate for military use. Muslim incendiary devices terrified the Crusaders. By the 15th century they had invented both a rocket, which they called a "self-moving and combusting egg", and a torpedo—a self-propelled pear-shaped bomb with a spear at the front which impaled itself in enemy ships and then blew up.

20 Medieval Europe had kitchen and herb gardens, but it was the Arabs who developed the idea of the garden as a place of beauty and meditation. The first royal pleasure gardens in Europe were opened in 11th-century Muslim Spain. Flowers which originated in Muslim gardens include the carnation and the tulip (The Independent March 11, 2006).

<u>1001 Inventions and the Library of Secrets</u>
In 2010, this film received twenty one
International Awards for excellence.
<u>1001 Inventions Exhibition London—BBC One News</u>

Thoughts and

Closing Summary

Throughout recorded history, the evidence is overwhelming concerning the ease with which mankind learns to be critical and make obvious the perceived faults and short comings of others.

Science News, Human Prejudice Has Ancient Evolutionary Roots Mar. 18, 2011 found at http://www.sciencedaily.com/releases/2011/03/110317102552.htm taken July 17, 2013 gives a strong explanation of the development of prejudice and bias.

I am deeply disheartened by how easily humans will spend hours each day creating arguments, dissention, and condescending talk and behavior against another, rather than spend a few moments learning from and about that other person or social group. How can humans be so GOD righteous and continue to debase another? For me, it is such a frightening mental trauma, to witness so many good deeds of individuals and groups who strive to do GOD's work, all the while carrying out the mission and goal of Satan. Does our ALL POWERFUL GOD need us humans to do HIS work? I'm sure not. I am sure however, we are invited in joining HIM, in HIS work.

So often, after a nice early morning rain, I have seen what I know as slugs, slowly making their way on the edge of a side walk. This sight causes me to compare all the vulnerable aspects and inabilities of such a lower life creature to myself. Then I imagine how much lower than GOD, humans are. Imagine one wet slug comparing itself to another (if they can or could). How capable is a slug to do my work? How capable am I to do GOD's work?

Reflecting back some number of years, the Bible Book of Ephesians, Chapter 6 stood out to me, specifically verses 10-17.

"<u>10</u> Finally, my brethren, be strong in the Lord, and in the power of his might.

<u>11</u> Put on the whole armour of God, that ye may be able to stand against the wiles of the devil.

<u>12</u> For we wrestle not against flesh and blood, but against principalities, against powers, against the rulers of the darkness of this world, against spiritual wickedness in high *places.*

<u>13</u> Wherefore take unto you the whole armour of God, that ye may be able to withstand in the evil day, and having done all, to stand.

<u>14</u> Stand therefore, having your loins girt about with truth, and having on the breastplate of righteousness;

<u>15</u> And your feet shod with the preparation of the gospel of peace;

<u>16</u> Above all, taking the shield of faith, wherewith ye shall be able to quench all the fiery darts of the wicked.

<u>17</u> And take the helmet of salvation, and the sword of the Spirit, which is the word of God:" (KJV)

Let each of us discipline ourselves to show respect to (ALL) our neighbors, and work to perfect ourselves to let GOD's love flow through us, and HIS love not be denied by our individual attempt to display imperfect human love.

Check out: "Experiencing God" By Henry Blackaby
At Amazon.Com